A VISION ACHIEVED

A VISION ACHIEVED

Fifty Years
of East Bay Regional
Park District

by
Mimi Stein

❦ EAST BAY REGIONAL PARK DISTRICT

Published by the East Bay Regional Park District for its Fiftieth Anniversary.

Printed in the United States of America by
Braun-Brumfield, Inc., Ann Arbor, Michigan
Design and Production: Matrix Productions
Typesetting: Vera Allen Composition

East Bay Regional Park District is grateful to the many photographers who photographed the parks over the years. Credit for some of the photos used in this book could not be determined, but those photographers who can be credited include: Sal Bromberger, p. 84; Jack Chinn, p. 50; M.L. Cohen, pp. 18, 24; Martin J. Cooney, pp. 53, 63, 67, 69, 74, 104; Cecil Davis, p. 68; A.J. Edwards, p. 38 bottom; Charles Haacker, pp. 72, 97; Andrew Ham, p. 25 bottom; Albert "Kayo" Harris, pp. 19 top, 21 left, 32, 35 bottom, 40 left and right, 42, 44; Ed Kirwan, p. 66 bottom; James La Cunha, p. 117; Luther Linkhart, p. 71; Nancy McKay, frontispiece, pp. 29, 58, 61–62, 75, 78, 82, 88–89, 94–95, 98, 100, 102–103, 105, 119; F.J. Monteagle, pp. 23 left and right, 36 right, 47, 52, 54, 64, 73, 81, 85, 106; *Motorland Magazine*, pp. 15, 33 bottom; Phil Palmer, p. 107; Dee S. Pruyn, p. 55; Kurt Rogers-*San Francisco Examiner*, p. 101; Mac Slee, p. 92; Louis L. Stein, Jr., p. 1; Cedric Wright, pp. v, 5, 6, 9; and A.E. Wieslander, p. 66 top.

ISBN 0-914531-00-x (cloth)
ISBN 0-914531-01-8 (paper)
1 2 3 4 5 6 7 8 9

Acknowledgements

To the people of the East Bay Regional Park District—area residents, park users, Board of Directors, employees, and staff—goes an overwhelming debt of gratitude, not only for making the parks possible in the first place, but also for their invaluable assistance in putting together this 50th anniversary commemorative book.

The District readily opened its historical files for research, and headquarters staff was unfailingly helpful and friendly in running down a myriad of details and dates. Special thanks should be expressed to Linda Chew and Sandra Stohler of the Development and Public Information Department, who supervised the entire project, to Harold Luhtala, Nancy McKay, Jane Gentile, and Rosemary Cameron for countless hours of locating photos, typing transcripts, and researching information, and to Edward MacKay and Seymour Greben for their editorial assistance.

For the full richness of the story we turned to people who built the District. In a series of tape recorded and transcribed interviews, conducted individually and in groups, 73 park pioneers, District long-timers, and community leaders shared their priceless recollections of and experiences with the District: the adventures, the challenges, the accomplishments, and the frustrations. Several also furnished photographs of the old days. Their assistance was invaluable; without it this book would not have been possible. A special thanks goes to them:

Robert L. Addington
George L. Allison
Richard J. Angel
Richard C. Aronson
Paul J. Badger
Anga Bjornson
Fred C. Blumberg
Joseph P. Bort
Lynn Bowers
Joyce Burr
George H. Cardinet, Jr.
Robert E. Clark
Arthur & Grace Cobbledick
Howard L. Cogswell
Edgar R. Collins
Jerome B. Collins
Walter H. Costa
Robert E. Daskam
Ellis Davis
Robert S. Davis
D.G. Dye
Harland Frederick
Andrew Gotzenberg
Ernest W. Hall
Marlin W. Haley
Paul E. Harberts
Dustin C. Heartsill
Stanley R. Hedlund
Ronald M. Holden
Charles R. Horbach
Hulet C. Hornbeck
James A. Howland
Mary Lee Jefferds
Robert H. Joyce
Robert I. Kahn
Jerry D. Kent

Catherine Kerr
Harlan Kessel
John T. Knox
John J. Leavitt
Thomas C. Lynch
Leila Macdonald
Sylvain H. Mahler
Frances Maiden
Richard B. Mauler
Lawrence O. McDonald
Milton O. McNeill
Raymond L. Middleton
Larry W. Milnes
Georgette Morton
William Penn Mott, Jr.
Arthur E. Navlet
John A. Nejedly
O. Christian Nelson
John O'Donnell
Mary L. & Harold L. Paige
Norman Pitchford
Jose N. Quintana
Ted Radke
Truman G. Rhoades, Jr.
Chester L. Scott
Glenn T. Seaborg
Carol Sibley
Grady L. Simril
Anthony Smith
Louis J. Testa
Carolyn Thatcher
Richard C. Trudeau
Charles F. Tronoff
Frederick Joe Williams
Clyde R. Woolridge

Grateful credit for invaluable research and writing assistance goes to Carole Hicke of Oral History Associates, for expert typing and transcription to Shirley Norman, and for the superb design and production to Matrix Productions. No project is possible without adequate funding, and a special thanks is due to The Robert Sibley Fund and the L. J. Skaggs and Mary C. Skaggs Foundation for their generous financial contributions.

Mimi Stein
Oral History Associates
June 30, 1983

Contents

*It is the main duty of government, if it is not
the sole duty of government, to provide means of
protection for all its citizens in the pursuit of happiness
against the obstacles, otherwise insurmountable,
which the selfishness of individuals
is liable to interpose to that pursuit.*
—Frederick Law Olmsted, Sr.

*If, as we generally believe, the primary asset
of this area is its quality of living, then it is vitally
important that we do our part to help to preserve
and improve these qualities, for without them we
simply become another community.*
—Richard C. Trudeau

Prologue

In 1772, four years before the thirteen North American colonies declared their independence, an intrepid Spanish missionary camped in what is now Tilden Regional Park. Father Juan Crespi was impressed with the beauty of this land, and noted in his diary the giant oaks and the abundance of deer, bear, and other game. His party also found a village of Costanoan Indians living in harmony with their surroundings.

The native bunch grass and the profusion of poppies and other wildflowers were described by later writers, who also mentioned a forest of giant Coast Redwoods, some so tall they served as landfalls for sailing vessels entering the fog-bound Golden Gate. Those ancient redwoods, however, were logged off during the mid-nineteenth century gold rush, and used to build the mushrooming city of San Francisco. The second growth was left largely undisturbed, foresting the hillsides with trees up to 18 feet in diameter. Dense thickets of mixed shrubbery—chaparral—covered much of the hills and canyons, interspersed with grassy valleys and clear, tumbling creeks.

As early as 1866 these hills behind Oakland and Berkeley captured the imagination of Frederick Law Olmsted, Sr., renowned U.S. landscape architect, who designed New York's Central Park. He suggested construction of "scenic lanes" over the Contra Costa hills.

In the bustle of post Civil War California growth, his vision went unheeded. Curiously, it would be water, and not the land itself, that many decades later would draw public attention back to his prophetic words.

The creeks flowing through the Contra Costa hills and the water table beneath the land had for many years provided the area's scattered residents with clear, bountiful water.

As the population grew, so did the need for more systematic development of water sources, and by about 1890, water companies had begun purchasing lands around Wildcat Canyon and digging wells to supply water.

Meanwhile, the scenic beauty of the watershed area continued to draw intermittent attention. In a 1906 study on the civic improvement of Oakland, Charles Mulford Robinson, well-known city planner, author, and journalist, urged the creation of parklands in the hills. Nine years later Dr. Werner Hegemann, another Oakland city planner, outlined a city plan for Berkeley and Oakland that called for parklands along the shore, within cities, and in the hills, where "beautiful sites like Wildcat Canyon must be held forever in a natural state and should serve the people for securing water and park reservations."

Like Olmsted's suggestion, these two reports were filed and forgotten, but the contoured hills and winding shorelines remained, forming an area of potential recreation and wilderness unparalleled anywhere else in the nation. There matters might have remained had not the growth of population in the 1930s and the resulting need for land for housing threatened to destroy permanently the wilderness area. When it became apparent that no existing public agency would accept responsibility for preserving the land, the citizenry, although caught by then in the throes of the Great Depression, developed a unique strategy for saving the hills and ridges for posterity.

1
Parks for the People: The District is Born

Creative vision and hard work by concerned citizens fashioned Frederick Law Olmsted Sr.'s "scenic lanes" into the precedent-setting East Bay Regional Park District. The strong cooperative effort of community groups and government agencies working closely together brought the visions of dreamers to fruition.

Land was the first ingredient needed to create the District. Thanks to the patchwork pattern of East Bay population growth—and the quirks of competition among early water companies—an abundance of watershed land was available to be set aside for recreational uses.

In the early years of the century, numerous small water companies had sprung up to service the scattered East Bay settlements. They secured their water by damming canyons on their lands to form cachement basins where the runoff water from the hills was collected and stored. Temescal, San Leandro, Chabot, and San Pablo were all old reservoirs that resulted from these efforts. Temescal was particularly important in that system because it was on the west side of the hills, and consequently a complicated pumping system was not required to bring the water over the hills into Oakland.

Since the source of supply depended on the cachement basins and reservoirs, each company vied fiercely with the others to tie up as much watershed land as it could and thereby keep it out of the hands of its competitors. By the 1920s, when competition in supplying water had proved to be inefficient and the warring companies had merged into

the East Bay Water Company, that company had amassed a vast acreage in the East Bay.

A severe drought in 1923 persuaded the voters of several East Bay communities that the local cachement basin/reservoir system of water supply was no longer reliable, and they opted to build a new system that would pipe water from the Mokelumne River in the Sierra to the East Bay. The East Bay Municipal Utility District was organized to accomplish this mammoth task.

Five years later, in 1928, EBMUD completed the consolidation of the water supply by acquiring the East Bay Water Company—and with it, its substantial landholdings. Determining that the small cachement basins were no longer necessary, the Utility District promptly declared these lands—some 10,000 acres—surplus and available.

"These Valuable Pieces of Land Ought to Be Preserved Forever."

The rush was on. Builders and developers were soon investigating the area with considerable interest. At the same time, the mere rumor that the wooded hills might soon be converted into manicured lawns and macadam galvanized outdoorsmen, who had fought unsuccessfully for years to open up at least part of the watershed area, into action.

Robert Sibley, Executive Manager of the University of California Alumni Association, was one of the prime catalysts. Hiking in the hills above Berkeley while recovering from an illness, he had grown to love those woods and streams. As his wife Carol recalled years later, "The day it was reported in the newspapers that the EBMUD was going to give up its holdings here in the hills, he went right down to city officials and said, 'These valuable pieces of land ought to be preserved forever.' "

The Campaign Gets Under Way

As a first move in this direction, Sibley and Hollis Thompson, Berkeley city manager, in about 1928 organized the East Bay Metropolitan Park Association. Its goal was to open these lands to the public as a chain of parks stretching 22 miles from Lake Chabot to Wildcat Canyon.

The Association was soon joined in this effort by other East Bay outdoors groups: Harold French and his Contra Costa Hills Club, the Sierra Club, the East Bay Planning Association, the Oakland Park League, the Oakland Recreation Commission, and other civic organizations. They petitioned EBMUD to set apart and maintain 10,000 acres as parklands, but the Utility District ignored their pleas.

Samuel C. May, Director of the Bureau of Public Administration at the University of California, was a linchpin connecting these diverse groups. As early as 1918 he had lectured his public administration seminars about the need to create parklands, and in 1930, when EBMUD had still not responded to the citizens' petition, he persuaded Oakland's Kahn Foundation to deposit $5,000 with the University of California to finance a survey of possible parks. Olmsted Brothers, a landscape architecture firm run by the sons of Frederick Law Olmsted Sr., and Ansel F. Hall of the Educational Division of the National Park Service were hired to do a comprehensive survey of the recreational needs of the East Bay communities. (The Olmsted firm had just completed a comprehensive survey and report for the newly organized State Park System.) To lend support to their efforts, the East Bay Regional Park Association was organized, consolidating several of the earlier park groups.

The Olmsted-Hall Report

Familiar with the area because he had already done a preliminary survey, Hall provided passionate inspiration. "His aesthetic appreciation for unspoiled natural beauty spilled over into an intense desire to share this world," recall Harold

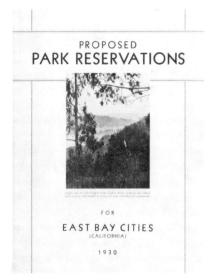

This survey made in 1930 by the Olmsted Brothers and Ansel F. Hall laid out specific plans and proposals for an East Bay park system.

and Mary Paige, both professional people living in the East Bay, who were close friends of Hall's. "We understood from Ansel that the regional concept was completely new and untried. We knew him as a dreamer, burning with enthusiasm for his innovative ideas and restless until he could get them planted into the minds of others with time, know-how, community influence and money to give them reality."

The 1930 Olmsted-Hall Report, a 41-page feasibility study that included maps and pictures, was a compelling statement of the need for parks. It urged EBMUD to open the lands, pointing out that the 150-square-mile area served by the Utility District, with its growing population of almost half a million, was far behind other cities in parklands. The Report, written over 50 years ago, offered what is sound park planning even today, emphasizing preservation of land that has multiple uses and is easily accessible. The authors did not envision then that the parks would be in the center of major urban areas. "As far as I know, it's the only regional

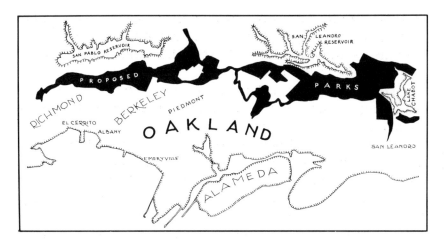

Map at left shows Olmsted-Hall proposed parks. A modern-day map of the East Bay area (below) shows the District parks at its 1936 opening.

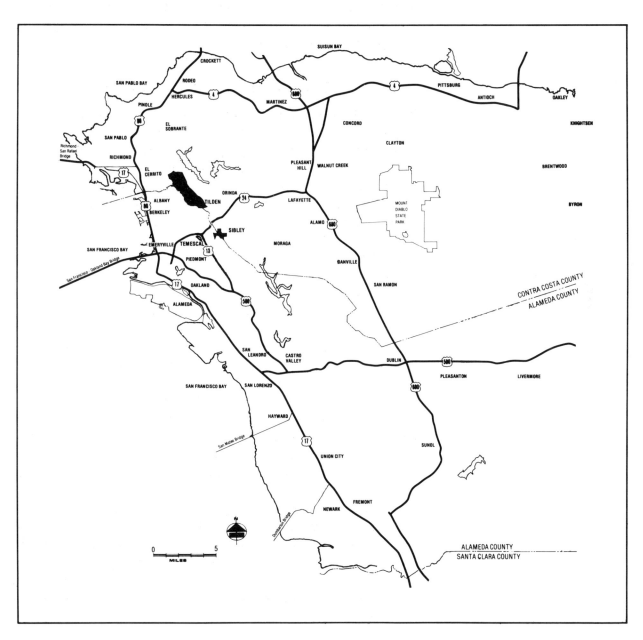

park system that is surrounded by the people it serves rather than being on the periphery. It's unique in the United States," comments Robert Kahn, whose father and uncle founded the Kahn Foundation.

The Report emphasized the need for sound, long-range planning, which remains an important element of the Park District administration to this day.

Envisioning a ring of parks surrounding the Bay, beginning with the East Bay hills, the Report prophetically warned about development filling along the bayshore, concluding that "a fair part of this shore should eventually be made accessible to the public." As it turned out, District acquisitions in the 1970s would follow these guidelines remarkably closely, and the prophecy about the value and beauty of shoreline sites would result in some of the most spectacular parks in the system.

A Regional Park District: A New Concept

Inspired by the Olmsted-Hall Report, more than 1,000 East Bay residents met on January 29, 1931, at the Hotel Oakland to sponsor the park project outlined in the report. Representatives of nine cities—Alameda, Albany, Berkeley, El Cerrito, Emeryville, Oakland, Piedmont, Richmond, and San Leandro—joined in petitioning EBMUD once again to create parklands out of the 10,000 acres of surplus watershed lands.

EBMUD at last reached a final decision. Already beleaguered by the task of supplying water to a growing community, its directors refused to take on the added burden of managing parks. The East Bay Regional Park Association—with some unexpected dissent from several of its influential members—was left with only one alternative: to call for the creation of a new government agency whose sole task would be to acquire and manage the parklands.

Inspired by the example of other California communities which during the 1920s and 1930s were pioneering the development of area-wide special districts to handle such problems as water supply that were beyond the capacity of traditional local government, East Bay park supporters proposed the formation of a regional park district that would include the nine-city, two-county area.

It was a unique and challenging concept. Although legislation already existed authorizing the special water districts, there was no precedent for a regional park agency. Overcoming these obstacles would require an intensive, region-wide drive and the cooperation of numerous city and county agencies, as well as a generous dash of panache and ingenuity.

A New Law

The first move was to bring together the mayors of the East Bay cities. "I had learned a lot about the local community back in '27 and '28 in a citizens' drive to organize the Bay Area cities," recalls Harland Frederick, who, as a student of Samuel May's, found the campaign dropped into his lap. "That effort failed because they didn't bring in the mayors and representatives of the various cities, and therefore those mayors opposed it. So when this came up, we were going to get the support of the mayors of every area so there would be no opposition. I was rather adamant on that."

The mayors of the East Bay cities were agreeable, and in March 1933 they organized a semi-official Regional Park Board under the chairmanship of Elbert M. Vail of Oakland.

Enabling legislation by the state of California would be required to establish a regional park agency. That meant persuading state legislators of the merits of this new idea. As Frances Maiden, longtime member of the Adelphian Club of Alameda, recalls, "Women's groups contacted assemblymen and senators, and we took them out to lunch when necessary." Citizens lobbying in Sacramento stressed the need for parks and recreation, as well as the employment this new agency would create for numbers of Californians on welfare rolls. As a further compelling argument, they pointed out that fire danger posed a threat to nearby cities if those lands were not protected and managed properly.

AB 1114, drafted by Assemblyman and former Oakland Mayor Frank K. Mott, and which authorized the establishment of a regional park district and a board to govern it, was passed in 1933—the same year that the state sales tax became law and California cast its vote for the repeal of Prohibition. On August 7, 1933, Governor James Rolph signed the bill, the first law of its kind in this country.

Citizens Roll Up Their Sleeves

The next step was to have the new District formally approved by the voters. This required an initiative petition to place a measure on the November 1934 ballot that would: approve the new District, elect a board of directors, and levy a tax of five cents on every $100 of assessed valuation to finance the District. Again the citizens rolled up their sleeves, collecting a grand total of 14,000 names.

At this point the campaign suffered its only setback. The Contra Costa County Board of Supervisors refused to sanction the election on the park initiative, causing El Cerrito and Richmond to withdraw their support. Most of Contra

Costa County at that time was rural farmland, and farmers objected to being taxed for parks—after all, this was the midst of the Depression—when they could find nature right outside their back doors. The Contra Costa County Board of Supervisors also feared it would remove too much land from the tax rolls. "It should not be necessary at this time to set up a new park department," commented a 1934 editorial in the *Richmond Independent*, "at the expense of the taxpayers, with spending powers it would be difficult to control once they were established."

DRUMMING UP SUPPORT: THE INVOLVED CITIZENS

Early visionaries—landscape architects and city planners—saw the need for preservation of beautiful scenery, but local residents sometimes had more down-to-earth reasons for wanting parks.

"I got interested in the parks for one main reason," recalls District Secretary Georgette Morton. "When we were kids we used to tramp these hills with no problems. Gradually the EBMUD was putting up fences and guards and wouldn't let us in. It made some of us a little bit mad."

She was not alone. Harold French, head of the Contra Costa Hills Club, campaigned aggressively for nearly 15 years to keep the hills open for hikers. He figured he wrote over a million words in his lifetime about parks—first to persuade EBMUD to create parks, then to promote the campaign for a separate Park District, then to smooth negotiations in the transfer of the acreage.

None of it could have happened without public support. Robert Sibley organized it; community leaders such as Robert Gordon Sproul, Fred Reed, and Major Charles Tilden, spoke in favor of it.

As the campaign swung into gear, other reasons for concern surfaced: "Most of us who were family-oriented wanted something for our children," observes Frances Maiden, a prominent member of the Adelphian Club of Alameda. "We liked to take them out on weekends for a little hiking or swimming. Recreation for the children was very important." Anga Bjornson, Oakland school teacher, adds: "I was just naturally interested in getting the parks because I spent my life as a teacher and I was always interested in anything that would give the children an opportunity to see a new phase of life and that would help do away with juvenile delinquency."

Volunteers worked tirelessly distributing flyers, telephoning, and getting out the vote. As Frances Maiden, who worked with women's organizations, recalls, "Toward the end of the afternoon, we'd find out who in each precinct had not voted. Then we'd come home, get the telephone book, and phone everyone who hadn't voted."

Others hit the streets. Union leader Tommy Roberts, who played a large part in getting out the organized labor vote, walked virtually every block in Oakland. "I personally give him much credit," says Bjornson, "for doing the necessary footwork. I've gone to labor union meetings when he stood up to speak, and they all listened, believe me. They knew that there was a man who had behind him the backing of the community. He was so well known and admired and respected."

When the Park District came into being, the Board of Directors continued the tradition of hard work and long-range planning by concerned citizens. "They were people who saw the future of this community as being connected with that park area," concludes Bjornson. "I thought it was advanced thinking for the community."

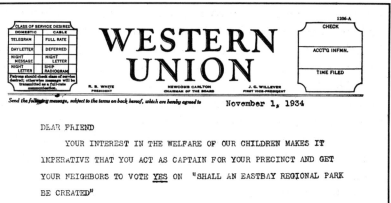

Send the following message, subject to the terms on back hereof, which are hereby agreed to   November 1, 1934

DEAR FRIEND

YOUR INTEREST IN THE WELFARE OF OUR CHILDREN MAKES IT IMPERATIVE THAT YOU ACT AS CAPTAIN FOR YOUR PRECINCT AND GET YOUR NEIGHBORS TO VOTE YES ON "SHALL AN EASTBAY REGIONAL PARK BE CREATED"

THE VOTERS DO NOT UNDERSTAND THAT THEY OWN THE LAND THEREFORE IT WILL COST THEM NOTHING AND THAT IN ORDER TO ENJOY IT THEY MUST VOTE YES. THIS MERITORIOUS PROJECT DEPENDS ON YOUR GETTING A MAJORITY YES VOTE IN YOUR PRECINCT.

E. M. VAIL, CHAIRMAN
REGIONAL PARK BOARD

As Chairman of the Regional Park Board, Elbert M. Vail solicited support for the ballot measure creating the Park District in 1934.

Alameda County Would Have To Go It Alone.

Next, a massive, get-out-the-vote campaign was organized to approve the ballot measure. A Committee of One Thousand urged a yes vote, which would, they proclaimed, create "parks for the people." Under Samuel May's direction, Harland Frederick set up campaign headquarters on the ground floor of the old Hotel Oakland. Spelling out the care taken to include the broadest range of community groups in the Park District campaign, Frederick recalls, "I sent cards to the president and secretary of every club in the entire East Bay asking them to be sponsors, and I got something like an 86 percent return—almost unheard of."

He solicited support from organizations as diverse as womens' clubs, the American Legion, the Retail Grocers' Association, real estate groups, and educational associations. Robert Gordon Sproul, President of the University of California, lent his prestige and immense energies to the effort. Nurseryman Arthur Navlet, who was president of the Oakland Downtown Merchants Association, added his enthusiastic support.

Mothers headed committees that canvassed house-to-house. Womens' clubs solicited every name in the telephone directory to get out the vote. They also served as forums for park organizers, such as Major Charles Tilden and realtor Fred Reed, who spoke at club luncheons, often addressing 300 or 400 people. "This was especially important," explains Mrs. Maiden, "since in those days we didn't have radio or television. These meetings were not just social affairs; they were a very important way of gathering people together." Reed's speeches emphasized that a park district would add to the value of homes and attract more people and businesses to the area.

"Vote for the East Bay Regional Park District in order that 'keep out' signs be replaced, legally, by 'come in' signs" proclaimed a Contra Costa Hills Club flyer.

Support flowed from city councils, schools, PTA's, churches, Scout leaders, and all manner of civic, commercial, labor, fraternal, and religious groups.

People with families were especially enthusiastic. Observes D.G. Dye, a San Leandro businessman, "We were looking toward the future to take care of our children and our children's children."

On the Saturday before the election, a 35-mile "get out the vote" parade rolled through Oakland with 12 floats showing outdoor sports, camping, and nature activities.

RECIPROCATING DIPLOMACY

The campaign to put the Park District on the map began a long tradition of inter-governmental agency cooperation that was nurtured for many years and has blossomed into a major District policy.

The University of California provided invaluable assistance. University President Robert Gordon Sproul buttressed the project, as did Alumni Association Director Robert Sibley. Several departments in the University rallied to the cause, especially the Bureau of Public Administration (now the Institute for Government Studies) then headed by Samuel May.

Professor May won help from the Kahn Foundation for the Olmsted-Hall study and kicked off the campaign with the help of graduate student Harland Frederick, who regards May as "the spark plug who pushed the whole thing through."

· Professors John Greggs and Harry Shepard of the Landscape Architecture Department added their support for regional parks, and the University also provided office space for Ansel Hall.

Hall, as a staff member of the National Park Service, was but one element in the Service's contributions to the infant District. The National Park Service was also responsible for overseeing the CCC work, which was so necessary to the park development. Other federal agencies, primarily the CCC, the WPA, and the PWA, also played an invaluable role.

In the campaign itself, the cooperation of the East Bay city governments proved vital, and the efforts of the many groups that lobbied and campaigned and canvassed door-to-door proved that the combined efforts of citizens working with their government agencies could be dramatically effective.

WHAT A NICKEL WAS WORTH

A vote for the proposed new park district in 1934 meant an increased five-cent tax on every $100 worth of property, an insignificant sum by today's standards, but in 1934 a nickel went a long way. Five cents in 1934 would buy a pound of apples. Two and a half nickels would buy a quart of milk. Coffee was 31 cents for a one-pound can, and pork roast sold for 9 cents a pound. A house in Oakland went for only $3,500. Yet many Alameda County residents barely had a nickel to spare. Of the county's population of 475,000, an estimated 50,000 were out of work. Despite the trying times, however, the area's residents had faith enough in the future and in the value of a nickel to cast their votes for open space and recreation.

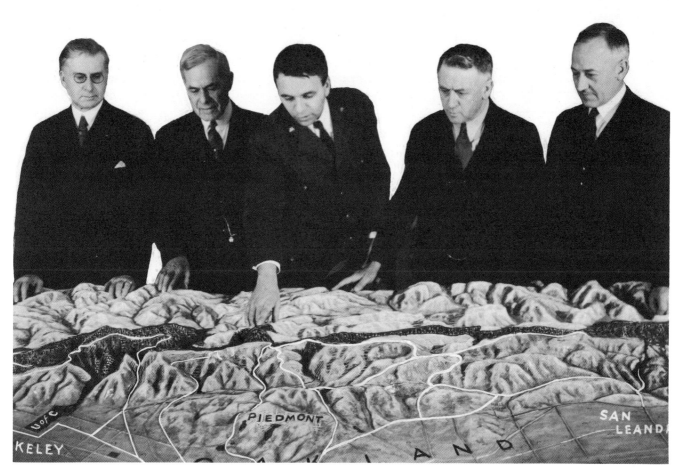

Ansel F. Hall of the National Park Service points out the proximity of the East Bay Regional Parks to the metropolitan area. Left to right: Mayors John McCracken of Oakland and E.N. Ament of Berkeley; Hall; Chairman William J. Hamilton of Alameda County Board of Supervisors; and Elbert Vail, General Manager, East Bay Regional Park District.

13

Excerpts from a 1934 flyer, which was part of the active campaign launched by East Bay citizens to form a park district.

The success of this hard-hitting campaign surprised even the organizers. On November 6, 1934, East Bay voters approved the park initiative by a vote of 2 1/2 to 1. It was a remarkable expression on the part of citizens who, undeterred by the economic hardships of the Depression, saw the long-range needs of their community.

On the same ballot, the voters also elected the Board of Directors: Major Charles Lee Tilden of Alameda, successful businessman, banker, and Spanish American War veteran; August Vollmer of the University of California, well known as Berkeley's police chief; Dr. Aurelia Henry Reinhardt, who had transformed a small, unknown school into Mills College, where she was serving as President; Leroy Goodrich, Oakland attorney; and labor leader Thomas J. Roberts.

Staff

The Board's first move was to appoint Elbert Vail as General Manager—without pay, at first. As Chairman of the Regional Park Board, he had helped shepherd the enabling bill through the legislature, then led the campaign to sign up thousands of petitioners and bring out the vote necessary to permit formation of the District.

General Manager Vail then hired the rest of the office staff: Georgette Morton, who had also begun as a volunteer. Her official title was Secretary and Treasurer, but she functioned as an all around Girl Friday.

The First Step: Land Acquisition

The fledgling Park District was now raring to go, but it had no land. Acquiring EBMUD's surplus watershed property was the Directors' first consideration.

A residue of rivalry left over from the years of agitation for EBMUD to operate parks complicated negotiations between the new Park District and the Utility District for land acquisition. The Utility District's President, former California Governor George Pardee, at first asked nearly $6 million for 10,000 acres, while the Park District offered less than $1 million. Park District President Major Tilden also stood unrelenting against the Utility District's demands for a bond issue to pay for the land. (Since the tax monies would come in dribbles, the Park District could not pay the entire price immediately.)

An independent appraisal was made at the request of the Park District, but still the Utility District refused to sell. In an effort to get things moving, Major Tilden advanced the

14

money for the Park District to buy 60 acres of privately held land in Redwood Canyon, obtaining it at a low figure—$35 an acre, to be exact—because of the Depression.

After several more rounds of jockeying back and forth, inter-agency diplomatic efforts finally resulted in a compromise, and in June 1936, the Park District purchased 2,166 acres for $656,544, or a little over $300 per acre. The recently enacted tax levy would pay for it over the course of the next five years, and as each increment was paid, "EBMUD was to cut its tax rate by that amount," wrote then-General Manager Elbert Vail, so that taxpayers did not have to pay for the land twice.

East Bay Regional Park District's new parklands included Wildcat Canyon (now called Tilden Regional Park), Roundtop (now called Sibley Volcanic Regional Preserve—which, it would be discovered four decades later, included the remains of an extinct volcano) and Lake Temescal. The shoestring park operating budget for 1936 totaled $194,835, but public interest in the parks was spreading.

At Last! The People's Playground

It was a time to celebrate, and the opening ceremonies held in Redwood Bowl on October 18, 1936 brought out the public in droves to enjoy a taste of the "peoples' playground." Harold French's Contra Costa Hills Club, which had invested 15 years of drumfire prodding and thus had a fair stake in this park system, conducted hikes to Redwood Bowl. East Bay riding groups mustered 300 Arabian, Thorough-

The contour of this hill, rising to 1,750 feet, gave the fitting name to Roundtop Regional Park (now Sibley Volcanic Regional Preserve) which encompasses it.

Redwood Bowl: above left, as an artist pictured it before it was built; above right, as the scene of ceremonies marking the official opening of the parks to the public in 1936.

bred, and Western horses with riders in costume, and the University of California marching band entertained, along with the Cal Glee Club and Treble Clef Society, massed choirs from East Bay high schools, and an R.O.T.C. battalion.

Major Tilden's 79th birthday furnished the occasion for another gala event that year, celebrated at the Claremont Hotel. Among the surprises awaiting him was the news that the former Wildcat Canyon Park had been renamed the Charles Lee Tilden Regional Park. It was hard to surprise the Major, however, because during that first decade, he missed only one board meeting. Taking advantage of his absence, the Board voted at that meeting to name Tilden Park in his honor.

Early Resources: Manpower

Meanwhile, Vail, now salaried—at $300 per month—mapped plans to take advantage of one of the few benefits to come of the Great Depression: the funds and manpower available to develop the parks through New Deal agencies—the CCC (Civilian Conservation Corps), the WPA (Works Progress Administration), and the PWA (Public Works Administration). In the agreement worked out with federal authorities, the government was to furnish 60 percent of the costs—mainly in salaries of the workers—and the Park District was to pay 40 percent, much of it in building materials donated by Utah Construction and Mining Company that were surplus after construction of the nearby Caldecott Tunnel between Alameda and Contra Costa counties.

Vail immediately authorized the construction of two CCC camps in Wildcat Canyon and launched a series of WPA projects which brought work to scores of the local unemployed. One of the first projects was Skyline Boulevard, providing a scenic drive along the ridgetop south of Tilden Park from which to view parts of the new Park District as well as the San Francisco Bay.

"Rain or shine, Director Tommy Roberts walked among the WPA workers, offering them encouragement," wrote Vail in his early history of the parks. "After the roads had been built, we began construction of caretakers' residences, office buildings, campgrounds, and restrooms."

CCC and WPA workers—with Roberts overseeing—cleared picnic sites, built tables and ovens, constructed playing fields, archery ranges, hostels for overnight campers, and a natural redwood amphitheater. These were made of unpainted redwood and stone quarried in the parks and were designed to blend unobtrusively into the natural scene. The administration building at Lake Temescal serves as a beautiful reminder of the distinctive stonework accomplished by those early workers.

CCC teams cleared hiking trails, bridle paths, and fire breaks. They found the poison oak a problem—sometimes half a crew would be put out of action—but their pay of $30 per month made up for the hazards.

The CCC, working with the National Park Service's State Park Division, also participated in the planning process. Arthur Cobbledick, distinguished Bay Area landscape architect, was assigned to the Lake Chabot CCC camp. Recalls

---

ARTHUR COBBLEDICK AND THE CCC

Landscape architect Arthur Cobbledick recalls an incident that occurred while he was supervising a CCC camp for the National Park Service.

"In one area, I was given permission to include a small nursery as a pilot project. We decided to favor native trees and shrubs and asked our work crews to call our attention to any unusual seeds or

acorns that might be of value or interest.

"Our superintendent was enthusiastic about this slight variation from the routine day's work and frequently brought in material for our consideration.

"At the end of one working day he approached me with a broad grin indicating that he had really found something.

The large seeds of this plant were a shiny black with conspicuous white blotches—truly something different.

"Imagine the look on his face when I informed him he was collecting *Rhus diversiloba*, Poison Oak! It would be only fair to admit that the plant was not in leaf at the time."

Forest, lake, valley, and mountains: a characterisitic scene in the Regional Parks.

Mr. Cobbledick, "I was given a copy of the original report put out by Olmsted and Hall. Emerson Knight, who was my direct superior, felt that this study was not adequate for the immense area concerned and that we could stand a more thorough study of the history of what turned out to be almost an empire." He and his CCC assistants spent the next four years mapping original trails, adobe homes, Indian sites, and lumber mills as part of the new report.

Organizing this wilderness into a recreation area called for much more water—water for people, water for plants, water for the golf course under construction. With the Public Works Administration providing half the funds, upper Wildcat Creek was dammed, creating Lake Anza, at a cost of $33,694.

Overall, in its formative first seven years, the District received an estimated $3 million in federally funded labor and materials, overshadowing revenues from tax receipts, which for those years totaled $1.7 million. The federal funds provided not only for the development of the parks but also for employment for residents of East Bay cities who had voted for them. It was a joint venture of mutual lasting benefit.

One of the unexpected benefits turned out to be the permanent park employees who came out of the CCC camps. The District's first field employee, Wesley Adams, originally had been hired in 1937 as liaison between the District and

The Civilian Conservation Corps camp in 1934. This later became the Tilden Nature Area.

To get the District started, Works Progress Administration workers, such as those pictured here, built roads, camping and picnic facilities, the golf course, rifle range, an archery course, and engaged in reforestation and drainage projects. Here WPA workers are building a rustic bridge on the fire control road in Redwood Canyon.

federal workers. Another later employee, James Roof, who headed the Botanic Garden for years, also came from the ranks of federal workers. "Without them the Park District could not have been developed," wrote Vail.

Tilden: *the* East Bay Regional Park

Gradually taking shape—a shape that would eventually make it *the* East Bay Regional Park—Tilden Park became an East Bay institution, a favorite of families and a refuge for students from the University of California campus.

Several of Tilden's most endearing and enduring features were the products of that first decade. In 1936 Billie Bell, well-known golf course architect, laid out an eighteen-hole championship golf course of varied fairways, challenging hazards, and well-clipped greens. Built with an old military tractor and opened in the following year, the golf course immediately became a popular recreation landmark and soon began to pay its way.

The first Annual Regional Golf Championship held at Tilden in 1937 began a tradition which has lured golfers from all over California every year; even boxing champion Joe Louis stepped off the tee for the 1945 tourney.

The clubhouse at the golf course opened in 1937—a "Nineteenth Hole" added much enjoyment to the game—and that same year Richard Walpole signed on as temporary "Green Keeper" at $40 a month. He would later move from superintendent of the golf course to the post of general manager of the District.

The Brazil Building arrived in Tilden by way of the World's Fair, held on Treasure Island in the San Francisco Bay in 1939. At the close of the Fair, Vail succeeded in persuading the Brazilian government to donate the interior of its Pavilion, with its burnished hardwood floors, plate glass mirrors, unique bamboo furniture, and wood-paneled walls. The WPA built a fitting stone exterior, making it one of Tilden's most-loved landmarks, and it opened in 1941 with fanfare and a catered luncheon.

At the same time, the District was beginning to establish the careful balance of recreational and wilderness features that would remain a hallmark of its parks to this day. Four and a half acres were set aside in Laurel Canyon as an area for growing plants native to California, a sort of "zoo" of native shrubs and trees for the public's education and enjoyment. Howard McMinn, Professor of Botany at Mills College, agreed to act as the District's botany consultant.

MAJOR CHARLES LEE TILDEN: "FATHER OF THE PARKS"

"He worked tirelessly for the creation of the parks," reported Elbert Vail, the first General Manager, "spending every Saturday checking on the many projects that were under way." These efforts and his name are rightfully memorialized in Tilden Regional Park, named in his honor on his 79th birthday in 1936.

Born in the California Gold Rush town of Chile Gulch, Major Charles Lee Tilden graduated from the University of California, took his law degree at Hastings College of Law, and distinguished himself in the Spanish-American War. During a long business career in the Bay Area, he involved himself in real estate, lumber, mining, shipbuilding, and drayage.

Instrumental in the founding of the Park District in 1934—often lending his prestige and speaking ability to the campaign—he helped forge a new government entity that was unique in design and effective in implementation.

He was nominated and elected to the first Board of Directors of the East Bay Regional Park District in 1934, and in recognition of his unstinting efforts in organizing the District, he was elected Board President. In that role he displayed an extraordinary talent for working with people. "The Major knew how to handle people without compromising himself or the issue," recalls Georgette Morton, the District's first secretary. "He'd let things go so far in the conversation, and when it got

hot, then he would have a way of cooling it down again."

Tilden was the prime mover in the Board's first goals: to acquire all available wilderness before it was lost forever, and to avoid burdening the community with a bonded indebtedness. His firm stand in the long and arduous negotiations with EBMUD over the acquisition of parklands was backed up by his own donations to the District of advance money to meet expenses and to buy its first land in Redwood Canyon. After he successfully negotiated the transfer to the District of what became Temescal, Roundtop, and Wildcat Canyon parks, he even dispatched a fleet of trucks to get the construction crews started.

He contributed his time and his can-do spirit to keep the District heading in the right direction throughout the remainder of the Depression and the war years. "He was a very civic-minded person," observes Leila Macdonald, whose husband, John, was on the Board for many years, "and was so interested in the parks that everybody always

enjoyed working with him."

Tilden continued to work diligently for the Board even when his energies were reduced by poor health. As Carolyn Thatcher, District secretary in the 1940s, recalls, "We used to have Board meetings in his bedroom, where he sometimes served sherry. His mind was clear; he carried out his Board duties just as well as ever."

The Major's contributions were recognized with frequent celebrations. Remembers Thatcher, "We used to have his birthday parties at the Brazil Building, with a luncheon at which local politicians and dignitaries would be present."

On his 93rd birthday—the 10th celebrated in the Brazil Building—the festivities included the unveiling of a bronze bust of Major Tilden created by Hilgar and Helen Webster Jensen. Placed on a column of natural stone in front of the Brazil Building, it formed a fitting tribute to his two decades of devotion to the District. He can truly be called the "Father of the East Bay Regional Parks."

The Brazil Building in Tilden Park, scene of parties for East Bay area groups for four decades.

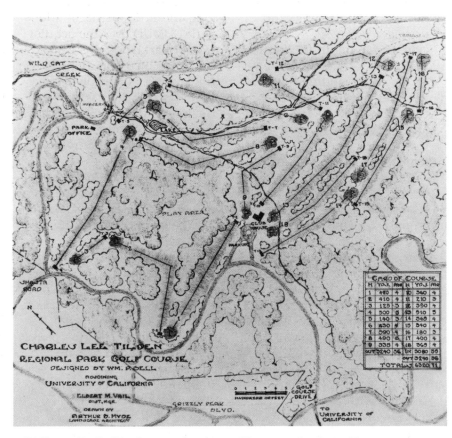

William P. Bell's design for the golf course built in Upper Wildcat Canyon (Tilden Park).

The Office

District administration was bare-bones. "Staff"—Vail and Morton—first occupied offices in downtown Oakland, but when the WPA completed the stone building and gardens at Lake Temescal in 1940, the District headquarters moved out there. Vail set policy and established direction, and Morton did everything else in the office. "The office was upstairs, and I was the office," she recalls, "and I just drove all over the place—in my own car, because we had no District cars"— downtown to pick up Secretary of the Board Roberts (he had to sign the checks); to the Bank of America where they kept the accounts; to the County Treasurer's office to pick up revenue from the latest collection of taxes.

With no budget for staff professionals, the District received advice on legal matters from Earl Warren, then Alameda County District Attorney, and on fiscal affairs from Fred Ferroggiaro of the Bank of America.

Redwood Regional Park Acquired

By the end of the decade, the District was ready to open its fourth regional park, Redwood. Earlier Major Tilden had advanced the money to buy 60 private acres in Redwood Canyon; then in 1939 the District agreed to pay EBMUD $246,277 for 1,494 acres densely covered with redwood trees, and shortly thereafter the park was opened with great fanfare.

Left: Lake Temescal administration building under construction.

Right: Finished beach and building at Lake Temescal.

Director Tommy Roberts (right) helps staff—Secretary Georgette Morton and General Manager Elbert Vail—move into new headquarters building at Lake Temescal in 1938.

LIFE AT HEADQUARTERS

As jill of all trades at the District's Lake Temescal headquarters, Georgette Morton found life required adaptability, but also offered certain amenities. "I was the only one in the office full time," Morton reports (Vail was out supervising work in the parks much of the time), "and we closed at noon for an hour. During the summer I'd put on a bathing suit—I had a little washroom there—and take a swim in the lake.

"We were on the second floor, and below us were the downstairs concessions. They put in a loudspeaker because I had a good view all over. If I'd see something wrong, I could call down to one of the lifeguards.

"One day—it was shortly be-fore the summer swimming season opened—two lifeguards were down at the lake getting things in order. I looked out the window and there was a little tyke about three feet tall on a tricycle on the beach. I called the boys' attention to him and asked them to bring him up to see who he was. They did, and he gave us his name: Bobby Beers. When I called the police, they said, 'Oh no, not him again!' Evidently, the little boy was a professional runaway."

She not only cared for lost children, she also facilitated communications. "The supervisors in the parks weren't near phones, and if it was something really important, I'd run out to tell them, be-cause I had a car."

Morton worked hard, but she found her job fascinating. "Many times we'd have childrens' groups that teachers would bring out to the parks. It was particularly pleasing to see the blind children. They'd have a rope, and each one would hold onto that rope. A teacher would be at the head and one was at the rear, and they walked them all around the lake. The teachers would describe everything, and you could just see happiness in those youngsters. They were absorbing all the things that we who see all the time never pay any attention to, and it meant so much to them.

"It was an interesting job. I never regretted any day I worked there."

Moved from the site of the 1939 San Francisco World's Fair, the Church of the Wildwood was the scene of many weddings before it was damaged and torn down within a few years.

John McLaren, builder of Golden Gate Park, who was acting as a consultant, hailed Redwood Park as the most beautiful natural park in the entire Bay area.

A tiny log cabin "Church of the Wildwood" was rescued from the World's Fair and installed at Redwood, providing a sylvan setting for services of all denominations. The first of many weddings celebrated in the church united Thomas Ryan and Josephine Aja in 1942.

Meanwhile, at Temescal Regional Park, the District faced the first of many struggles against attempted incursions in the years to come when it successfully averted an extension of Mountain Boulevard that would have threatened the park.

"No Municipality Has Accomplished So Much With So Little"

The decade's end was also an appropriate time to assess the District's progress and consider its goals for the future. Shortly before he retired as General Manager, Vail drew up a Master Plan—the first of the District's many long-range plans—for the '40s, in which he outlined the work to be done. He also took the opportunity to consider the past with

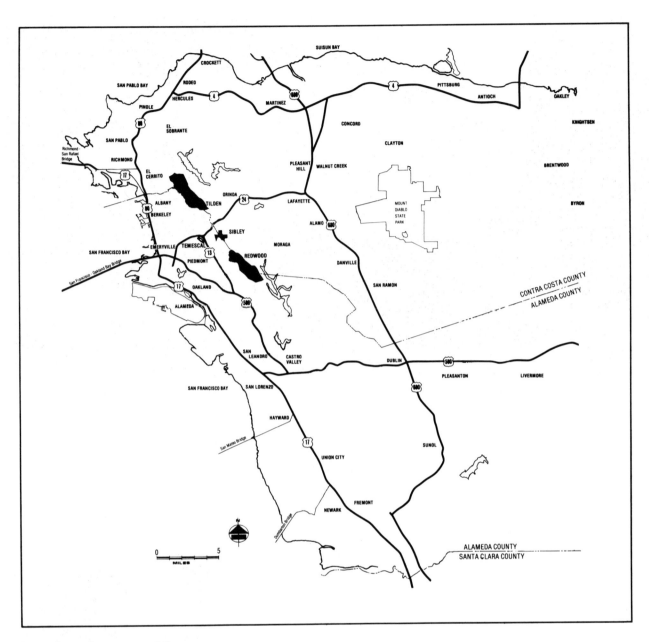

A modern-day map of the area shows the extent of the District parklands in 1940 at the end of Elbert Vail's term as General Manager.

pride. Despite a crippling economic Depression, area residents had voted to tax themselves for parklands. In just four years of intensive work and bare-bones budget, four regional parks totaling approximately 4,000 acres had opened. The 48-acre Lake Temescal Regional Park was at the District's geographic center and was the site of administrative headquarters. Scenic drives connected the three other parks— Charles Lee Tilden, 1,890 acres, Roundtop, 228 acres, and Redwood, 1,554 acres.

The Park District encompassed 18 miles of roads, 21 miles of trails, 12 play fields (including a cricket field used for the San Francisco World's Fair Championship cricket

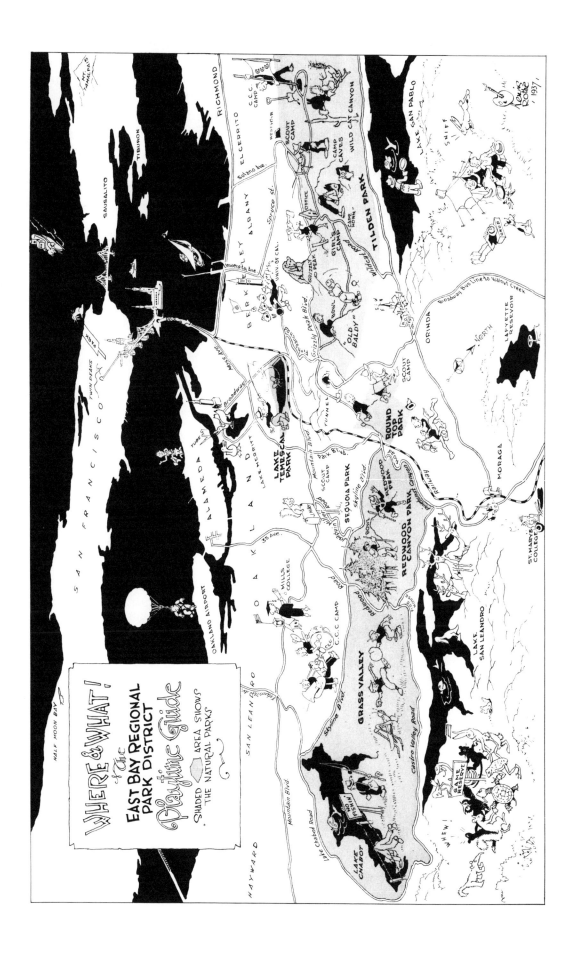

matches), 2 beaches, and dozens of other recreational and sports sites and wilderness areas. Over one million people used the parks each year, taking advantage, as Vail noted, of the "great variety of hill, valley, forest, and plains, and the easy accessibility to all parts of the suburban area."

Striking an early resource-conservation note, his Plan stated that "thousands of dollars will be saved yearly by the capital outlay for water storage, rock plant, and other investments to utilize the natural sources within the parks."

"No municipality," he concluded with pride, "has accomplished so much with so little."

2
Cautious Expansion: The Walpole Era

Pearl Harbor ended all hopes of continuing the infant District's growth spurt. Park manpower and resources were drastically reduced as they were redirected to the war effort—the CCC and WPA workers were withdrawn entirely—and the District modified and curtailed its operations to meet new and stringent conditions.

The military created new demands. President Franklin D. Roosevelt called upon all recreation agencies to "strengthen your services in behalf of the young men in the armed forces." The District immediately offered about 500 acres in Tilden Park to the Army Defense Command.

The army, pleased with the suitable terrain, used the woodlands for survival training and overnight bivouacs. Abandoned CCC barracks became a rest camp for convalescing soldiers, while the Fourth Air Force used the site of the current Tilden Service Yard as the nerve center for 15 watchdog radar stations. In the years after the war, when park workers inspected the old blockhouse, they found a windowless, nearly bomb-proof room, with a half circle on the floor marking where the desks had been, and a large map of the world on the opposite wall.

Both the Park District and the army benefited from this arrangement. The District provided hard-to-get facilities for recreation, training, and defense—high spots like Vollmer Peak were ideal for observation and communications—while army troops cleaned up trails, trimmed poison oak, cut trees, built bridges, and erected signs. GI patients at the rest camp painted buildings, weeded, hoed, and sawed wood.

Covering All Bases

It was well they did, for the Park District needed all the help it could get. District General Manager Harold L. Curtiss, who replaced Elbert Vail when he resigned in 1942, faced the challenge of the gradual decline of operations, as many of the District's employees went off to fight the war or take positions in critical defense industries.

As their numbers dwindled from 30 down to 6, the remaining few workers had to cover all bases—maintaining and policing 4,100 acres of public lands, $4 million worth of improvements, and 20 miles of roads which had to be kept in a state of availability for evacuation.

At the same time, the Board of Directors, in a budget-cutting move, reduced the work week from six to five and a half days, and although they discussed the possibility of training women to fill the vacancies, nothing came of it.

Wesley Adams was one of those who stayed with the District—he was deferred from military service because the army needed him in the parks. He was left with only one assistant—his wife—to run the entire Redwood Park. She took reservations for the lodge and even helped him fight fires. Occasionally in fire-fighting they got a helping hand from bartenders of the several taverns along Redwood Road. Adams' original fire truck was a 1932 Studebaker touring car—painted red, but with no bell, lights, or siren. In the back

During the World War II years, the U.S. Army used the old Civilian Conservation Corps buildings as barracks.

seat he carried a 50-gallon drum of water with a belt-driven pump and a garden hose.

Fire was a problem. Disasters, such as the near-hurricane in 1944 which started a fire, wreaked havoc in the parks. The six workers were hard pressed.

Still, the staff made do with what they had. They kept the parks open, and new rhododendron and azalea gardens were planted at Temescal, the annual tree-planting program was continued, and some parcels of property were acquired. Civilians continued to enjoy their favorite facilities. In 1942, for example, the always-popular Brazil Building served as luncheon site for 75 recreation directors attending the National Recreation Association's Western Division Conference. The Shipyard Workers held a Labor Day picnic; swimming, boating, and fishing continued at the lakes; and there were weddings at the Church of the Wildwood.

The Board of Directors not only cut hours, but—in keep-

Horseback riders at the Spruce Gate entrance to Tilden Park in 1943.

WARTIME AT REDWOOD

Jim Howland, Park Supervisor, who started to work at the District in 1962, is a third generation park employee. His grandfather went to work for the District in 1939, and his father signed on in '41. From 1943 to 1951, the Howland family lived at Redwood Bowl.

"I remember living there during the war years," recalls Howland. "There was an anti-aircraft battery up near where the main office is now. A grave registration training battalion was over by East Ridge Trail. I remember looking across from Redwood Peak down on East Ridge Trail. I'd see a new cemetery every week. That is where they would practice digging graves, setting them up, and grading them out.

"Another thing I remember as a kid: There was a two-week survivor training program which pre-flight stu-dents went through. This was always at Redwood Park. At the end of the course, they were given one basic C ration unit per day and sent out to try to survive on whatever they could find at Redwood. I remember they would always wind up at Redwood Bowl. The instructor would always make sure my mother had a pound of coffee on hand—it was hard to come by then—so that she would be sure to have a hot pot of coffee ready for these guys as they'd straggle through after two weeks of survival training.

"And what I loved about having them there was that most of these guys would save their little chocolate bars and C rations for me. All I saw of chocolate through the war years was what I got from them."

ing with overall wartime belt-tightening—reduced the nickel tax rate to three cents soon after the war started, further lowering it to two cents in 1945. Careful management, however, kept the District in good financial shape throughout the period, and by the end of the war, $300,000 had been saved out of tax monies and put into war savings bonds, and an additional $200,000 had been accumulated in the general fund.

New Growth at War's End

The return of peace in 1945 ushered in a new era of prudent growth and consolidation for the Park District under the leadership of Richard Walpole, who replaced Curtiss that year. A large, strong man with a commanding voice, Walpole already had eight years' experience with the District. For most of that time, he had been manager of Tilden Golf Course, and he continued to give it considerable attention.

Golf attracted many visitors to Tilden, and the District's tournaments—one southpaw golfer even started a yearly championship for left-handed players—stirred public interest and attracted golfers from all over the country. The golf course offered an additional contribution: it paid its own way.

Richard Walpole, left, appointed General Manager in 1945, watches as Lake Temescal is planted with black bass and bluegill fish.

Tilden Park's manicured greens and rolling fairways have challenged golfers from all over California—and the nation—since it opened in 1937.

LIVING BRIDGES

From its earliest beginnings, the District has always tried to make use of equipment and materials at hand. Often the raw materials came from the parks themselves, but sometimes there were unexpected consequences.

Jim Howland, third generation park employee, grew up in Redwood Canyon when his father was working for the District. As a youngster in the early '40s, he watched park workers cutting hiking trails bit by bit through dense redwood groves.

"In order to cut the redwood trees," he recalls, "they would have to build a road in. It was during the war when concrete and steel weren't available, so

in order to make bridges, they would split the trees and lay them across the stream.

"Of course, they couldn't work in the winter, and when we came back in the spring, all the bridges were growing profusely. The freshly cut redwood had been put back into the moist soil where it was heavily shaded, and the cut end had just taken root. It was quite a sight.

"The District finally decided they would have to treat the timber to keep it from growing, or we would have living bridges."

On the other hand, the course also required untold hours of upkeep. Early maintenance crew workers recall endless nights spent watering the fairways and greens. Eddie Collins, now Supervisor at Temescal Regional Recreation Area, went to work in 1946 watering the course every other night. "Water was pumped from Lake Anza," he recalls, "into a reservoir in back of the golf course, and it was gravity-fed back down to the course."

If there wasn't enough rainfall, they used water from the water company's next-door reservoir. But if there was too much rain, landslides wiped out the eight-inch pipe that carried the water. Grady Simril, hired as night waterman in 1949, remembers that making the rounds to turn on the water valves with Bob Davis, who broke him in, required the speed and endurance of a track star. "He ran all night long. He would turn one water valve on, and he'd run back to another section of the course and turn the other off, because at that time the faster you could get back to turn the other one off, the more pressure you got."

"We Had One Screwdriver and One Wrench Between Us"

As always, after the watering came the mowing—an endless cycle in the struggle to grow grass—and even during the winter, the pace continued with necessary repairs to be made. As Larry McDonald, who started as a park worker in 1948 "when hamburgers were fifteen cents," recalls, "Eddie Collins and I had to repair the mowers during the winter months. We had one screwdriver and one wrench between us"—and they brought those from home. "We would service about 25 mowers during the winter months. Then we would get all the sprinklers and broken water lines repaired, fertilize the golf greens, and cut wood after a big rainstorm would come through.

"Pappy Waldorf's football team from Cal came during the holidays to work—they were in training—and they helped us cut wood and manicure the greens." In turn, a whole row of East Bay Regional Park District people accompanied the team when it went to the Rose Bowl in 1948.

The number of park visitors, which had fallen off during the war, now surged ahead, rising from half a million in fiscal year '44–'45 to over two million in '47–'48.

Normal summer weekends found people picnicking in the parks, playing tennis, flying model airplanes, swimming in Lakes Temescal and Anza, and listening to recorded concerts from the Brazil Building.

The first annual Junior Horse Show and Parade in 1948 was held at Tilden Regional Park. Tom Flood, Assistant General Manager, is shown talking to costumed contestants.

34

The Merry-Go-Round and Other Concessions

To meet the growing demand, in 1946 the Board of Directors voted to resume the full nickel tax and launched plans for more recreational facilities. Two years later, the District opened a new attraction for children—of all ages—that is still a District landmark, the Tilden Merry-Go-Round.

Negotiations for the carousel had started some time back. Leila Macdonald remembers that her husband, John, who had been appointed to the Board in 1945, traveled with General Manager Walpole to Los Angeles to see Ross Davis, the famous merry-go-round entrepreneur, about acquiring one for the Park District, the first in the East Bay. Davis agreed to install one in Tilden Park, a vintage carousel built in 1911 by the Hershell Spillman Company. Davis' son-in-law, Harry Perry, came along as operator, and his enthusiasm added greatly to the fun. Landscaping of the area was planned by Andrew Gotzenberg, noted East Bay landscape architect, who also helped plan the golf course's sprinkling system.

The real merry-go-round enthusiasts, however, were the hundreds of thousands of children, parents, and grandparents who rode it. Not only was it a popular amusement ride, it was—and is—a work of art, with its full complement of hand-painted, wooden, carved animals—all of which are now antiques.

Perry and his partners, Ross and John Davis, owned the

This was an era when everyone did everything: General Manager Richard Walpole designed this plan for the Merry-Go-Round area, and Secretary Carolyn Thatcher executed the drawing.

When the Tilden Park Merry-Go-Round was dedicated on May 29, 1948, staff and members of the Board of Directors took time off from the ceremonies to enjoy a whirl on the popular attraction.

Happiness is a pony ride at Roberts Park.

The Little Train—a 1½-mile ride enjoyed as much by grown-ups as by children—is modeled after old-time narrow gauge equipment. Built to a scale of a little less than half size, the present-day concession has two locomotives: one, #4, patterned after logging and mining locomotives of the 1875 era, and the other, #11, patterned after a combination freight and passenger engine of about 1900.

carousel until the mid-1970s, when the Park District acquired it—lock, stock, and barrel organ—and restored it. It was subsequently listed in the National Register of Historic Places. Perry now operates it under a concession agreement.

Within a few years after the arrival of the merry-go-round, the Board launched several additional concessions—all operated by private individuals: the pony ride, the steam railroad, and a trout pond.

Trucks, Trailers, and Tractors

Not all the tax nickels went for more facilities. In 1947 the Board earmarked some of the funds for purchasing war surplus equipment.

The story of the District's equipment goes back to the '30s, when Major Tilden donated several trucks, including two Kleibers and two Macks. Supplementing this windfall, the District in 1937 purchased its first tractor—a vintage machine that had been used in the construction of the nearby Caldecott Tunnel.

Hauling road-building rock into Redwood Park from a quarry in Tilden, District crews found that this ancient machinery—which would have been more appropriate in an exhibit at the Smithsonian Institution than at work in the District—made the going tough.

"We had an old front-end loader," recalls Grady Simril,

36

"but the tracks would come off and we would spend half the day fixing it."

The state of the old equipment and the new postwar growth clearly required additional machinery.

Clyde Kelsey, District purchasing agent, seized every opportunity to obtain war surplus trucks and earth-moving machines, at far less cost than new equipment. Among his acquisitions were a front-end loader, dump trucks, trailers, a cement mixer, and two Caterpillar tractors.

Since fires were always a major concern, Kelsey rounded up old airport crash trucks—two Internationals and a Dodge—for use as fire trucks to replace Wes Adams' old Studebaker touring car. "The golf course workers did most of the fire fighting for the District," recalls Eddie Collins, who went to work for the District in the mid-'40s. "Bob Clark (who headed the service yard) was the Fire Chief, and I was the fire boss for about 12 years. Whenever we had a fire anywhere in the District, we set off a siren at the service yard that could be heard in all of Tilden Park, and everybody would drop whatever they were doing, grab the fire trucks, and go out and fight." Local fire departments also often lent a hand.

The Park District Grows

A major element of the new growth was the acquisition of more lands. First, some parcels of property surrounding Redwood Regional Park were added for a total of $120,000 to round out the holdings in that area, but that was only a start.

Bob Sibley, who had been appointed to the Board in 1948 and served as President from 1949 until his death in 1958, would usually spend two afternoons a week with Dick Wal-

---

PURCHASING IS NO EASY JOB

As Purchasing Agent, Clyde Kelsey wielded considerable power, but his job entailed some tough decisions: for the most part, Kelsey leaned toward few, rather than many, expenditures. Employees figured that when they put in an order for tools, he would automatically halve the order. That is, if he ordered them at all.

Knowing all that, Eddie Collins, now Supervisor at Temescal Regional Recreation Area, doubled his order for tools. Kelsey at first protested that the tools would not be properly cared for, but finally he relented and agreed to handle Collins' order.

"I had ordered twice as many as I wanted," recalls Collins, "and I guess I did such a good job of convincing him that he doubled the order. A few weeks later he went back and doubled the order again—apparently he had found a good buy—and suddenly we had more mattocks and crowbars than we knew what to do with. That sure kept us going for a good, long time."

Roberts Regional Recreation Area opened to the public in 1953; it provides swimming, volley-ball, play fields, trails, and picnic areas at the north end of Redwood Park.

Checking the plans for the new Roberts Regional Recreation Area are Directors Robert Sibley, John Macdonald, General Manager Richard Walpole, and Director Tommy Roberts, for whom the park was named.

pole looking at what lands were available and what could be done to improve the parks.

One of the parcels they found was an 88-acre area next to Redwood that the District transformed into a recreational unit with picnic areas, merry-go-round, pony ride, a ball field, and a swimming pool. Opening in 1953, it was named the Thomas J. Roberts Regional Recreational Area in honor of the union man who had stumped for the birth of the District, watched over it during its early years, and still remained an active Board member.

Another area that attracted the Board's attention was a beautiful valley known as Grass Valley, owned by the East Bay Municipal Utility District. The original plan made before the District was formed called for acquisition of 959 acres in Grass Valley. EBMUD priced the land at $225,000 and began lengthy negotiations with the Park District. Although the Utility District attached several restrictions to the Condition of Sale concerning adequate protection of drinking water in its reservoir, the Park Board members could see the importance of recreation for East Oakland, San Leandro, Hayward, and Castro Valley residents, and they bought it anyway.

The Park Board and staff met with the local citizens as well as EBMUD officials, even holding a barbeque in 1951 to acquaint the public with the new facility. Later named Anthony Chabot Regional Park after the pioneering engineer who built the Lake Chabot dam in the nineteenth century, the new Grass Valley park opened in 1952.

THE BARBEQUE TRADITION

The East Bay Regional Park District had always loved a good show, and when the time came to acquaint the local citizens with what would become Anthony Chabot Regional Park, a public barbeque was planned. It was actually a year before the park opened: 1951.

"I had once been a cook," recalls Grady Simril, presently Horticulture Specialist. "I had started doing the picnics for the District, and I offered to do this big cookout. That meant I had to spend a day with Clyde Kelsey, the Purchasing Agent, and that was an education in itself.

"That's how we got the 20-foot barbeque stoves. We went out and found material so that I could make the stoves—we used house brick—and we built the pits down in what was then Grass Valley. We built two 20-foot stoves.

"We worked all that night. I don't remember a person who refused to work. I think Bill Sass was running the water truck, and we had the whole District work force there.

"We had one big, flat-bed truck that we used to haul everything in. I think the only thing we contracted out was the salad: someone else brought that.

"We cooked and served all the mayors and all of these people in the District."

Grady cooked up a lot of enthusiasm as well as hamburgers, and he was still doing it in 1982, when he presided with skill and a hearty smile over a barbeque stove (this time it was portable) to welcome people to the newly restored Crown Memorial State Beach.

It was the sort of park where, after only a short drive, people could camp for two or three days in a wilderness setting, and it provided a nice balance to the highly developed recreational parks like Tilden.

The acquisition of Grass Valley brought regional parks to south county areas that were not a part of the District. Concerned about their share in developing the new park, residents of Eden Township voted in 1956 to annex themselves to the District, and two years later Washington Township followed suit. The tax base was thus broadened to ensure that those who used the parks the most helped to pay the cost.

The Nature Area

Development in north county parks continued to focus primarily on Tilden Park. The old CCC barracks, now emptied of convalescent soldiers, became a year-round nature study area. Under a $4,200 grant from the Rosenthal Foundation,

The Districts first naturalist, Jack Parker, demonstrates that it is all in knowing how to handle animals.

Jack Parker moved in as the resident naturalist, with his wife Martha as his assistant. Establishing a small interpretive center in the old, battered buildings with exhibits from the Oakland Museum and the State Fish and Game Commission, Parker also set up a Junior Ranger program for 8-12 year olds, who came in every Saturday morning. "Parker would take these kids out in the woods rain or shine," recalls Chris Nelson, now Chief of Parks and Interpretation. "His rule was that you held your hand out, and if you could see your thumb, you went." Sometimes the thumbs were wet with rain, but the children trooped along with gusto.

The local schools—Oakland, Berkeley, Albany, and Emeryville—set up their own nature programs, hired their own staff of two people, and worked out of one of the CCC shacks.

Another popular feature of the Nature Area was the Little Farm, built in 1955 with funds donated by the Berkeley Kiwanis Club. The Little Farm teemed with a menagerie of chickens, geese, ducks, and burros, plus a pig, two caracul lambs, a nanny goat and two kids. Youngsters visited the miniature red barn to see the baby animals.

40

Something For Everyone

Reaching from Tilden in the north to Grass Valley in the south, the District now offered something for nearly everyone: hiking, horseback riding, train rides and model trains, a cricket field, flycasting, archery, and a native plant Botanic Garden. Under the care of James Roof, the Botanic Garden displayed an outstanding collection of California native plants, and its friends were both vocal and enthusiastic. Roof was a plant genius, gathering, nurturing, and displaying plants illustrating a wide variety of California ecosystems.

Some of these activities—the carousel, the train ride, the clubhouse at the golf course—were managed by concessionaires. "Mr. Sibley was interested in being sure that the concessions were the right ones," reflects Carol Sibley, "that they would not invade the park in a way that would take away its naturalness. Bob was a great dreamer, and his ideas were to keep the parks in excellent condition, add land, make sure that the people who had the concessions kept them

Picnickers put on the coffee pot at Lake Anza.

"REPORT TOMORROW"

"Hiring people in those days," recalls Chris Nelson, Chief of Parks and Interpretation, "was done by what I call the 'one foot on the running board' method. If you were looking for work, you walked up to a guy in a park truck and stuck one foot on the running board—which they had back in those days—and asked him for a job. If he had a job open, he said, 'Sure. Report tomorrow.' "

Sometimes it was lucky that the park trucks had running boards.

For instance, as Nelson tells the story, Josh Barkin, out hiking in the woods, met a youngster who asked him where he was going with his pack. (Barkin had just quit his job in a lamp factory back East.) "Oh, I'm just taking a

Josh Barkin in action with a group of fascinated potential naturalists.

hike," replied Barkin."Going off to seek your fortune?" asked the child. Josh thought to himself, "I think, by golly, I'll do just that." He turned the corner up at Skyline, made a beeline to the District office,

asked for a job, and got it. Although he started out cleaning restrooms, "very shortly," concludes Nelson, "he was on his way to becoming one of this state's most famous and best naturalists."

Shown at the 1953 opening of the Boy Scout shelter at Tilden are left to right: Charles Warner, Carl Mack, Park Director Robert Sibley, and General Manager Richard Walpole.

within the spirit of the park, and hopefully have the parks be used and used and used."

Those were the goals of the early founders—Bob Sibley among them—and they continued to inspire staff and the Directors.

To meet the growing popularity and use of Tilden and the newer parks, the District's work force began to expand, and the office paper work grew proportionately. Carolyn Thatcher, who joined the District in 1946 as Secretary and Girl Friday, measured the increase in business by watching how the stack of time sheets thickened. "We started with a little stack, and the next year it was a little bigger, and pretty soon it was quite high."

Everyone Did Everything

Much of this increase, however, was simply refilling the gaps left by the war years, and now barely met the needs of the rapidly increasing East Bay population. By necessity, everyone at the District did everything, with remarkable flexibility and ingenuity. Parker, the naturalist, also did surveying. Carolyn Thatcher not only kept the time sheets and the books but also mapped the wards, redesigned the new headquarters building—"In the original design, there was no stairway to go from upstairs to downstairs," she chuckles—and drew up complete plans for a couple of parks, enabling the Alameda County Flood Control and Water Conservation District to get funds for two proposed dams—Cull Canyon and Don Castro.

In the field, maintenance crews displayed their versatility as they battled tree stumps, lack of tools, recalcitrant machinery, overtime without pay, and Walpole's fire drills.

Citizens' groups in the nearby communities lent a helping hand. The Park District's first outdoor shelter was dedicated in 1951 by the Fruitvale Lions Club, and the Kiwanis Club donated a grove of redwoods. Members of the Oakland Real Estate Board held a "Know Your Regional Parks Day" in 1948. Starting with a parade from downtown Oakland, they continued to Tilden for a day of picnicking, swimming, golf, tennis, dancing, horseshoe contests, and a barbecue.

Safety: A Constant Concern

The increased public involvement with the parks made public safety one of the District's major priorities. The parks were as safe for the public as possible, because insurance broker Percy Ramsden toured the parks and reported haz-

THOSE WERE THE DAYS . . .

Those were the good old days when everyone did everything, unfettered by red tape and paper work that came with advanced organization. (Walpole might send out a memo two or three times a year.)

A large, daily dosage of ingenuity was part of the job requirement. "I couldn't get the parts I needed, so I fabricated them myself," reports retired mechanic Bob Davis, recalling the time he installed power steering on an old Reo truck. "I pulled a fan belt from something else and made a pulley for my compressor. There were lots of times when auto parts would be too long in coming. I'd go to the scrap iron pile and find something in there and just make what I needed."

Park workers Milt McNeill, Tom Lynch, and Francis Kabeary prided themselves on constructing from scratch one-and-a-half picnic tables—a 4 × 4 plank table with concrete legs—in a day. "We'd dig the holes in solid sandstone with no power equipment, completely set the concrete legs, cut all the lumber, plane it down, and give it a coat of logwood oil at the same time," reports McNeill.

The flip side of the self-sufficiency coin was a high degree of autonomy. "We followed the Public Resources Code sections that pertained to regional park districts," reports District Secretary Carolyn Thatcher, "but there wasn't anybody telling our Board what to do."

The area of parklands was smaller then, more easily managed.

Those were the days when the District was still small enough to host summer barbeques and Christmas parties for all employees and their families, and the entire group could fit into the Brazil Building, with room left over. (It was quite a contrast to when, at last count in 1982, permanent employees numbered 350, with 210 temporary/seasonal workers.)

Those were the days when the local horsemen planned a three-day trail ride entirely within park limits. (By the 1970s, the District would have expanded enough to allow a seven-day ride.)

Everyone knew everyone else, and the camaraderie was matched by a sense of pride in work well done. Park Supervisor Dick Mauler puts it this way: "When we went out there, we saw what needed to be done and we pitched in and did it. I remember at Redwood, many times we never took breaks; and we'd work ten or twelve hours a day sometimes and never even think of overtime."

Those days are gone, but they are worth remembering.

ardous conditions—where guard rails or signs were needed, for example.

As with fire fighting, the District had safety protection from the community, too. "Any time we had trouble on the beach at Temescal," recalls Charlie Tronoff, retired Manager of Crafts Maintenance, "we'd get on the phone, and within minutes an Oakland police officer would be there." In return, the District offered the Police Officers' Association the use of the Temescal clubhouse to hold its meetings.

In other safety measures, the Alameda County Health Department counted the bacteria in the swimming waters every week. Occasionally the count would exceed acceptable limits because of the mud hens and ducks, and then the water would be treated with copper sulfate. Each year a Red Cross executive trained a new crop of lifeguards for the beaches.

WALPOLE'S FAMOUS FIRE DRILLS

Fire fighting in those days was everyone's responsibility. The old Internationals and the Dodge—former airport crash trucks—carried all the necessary equipment, and the procedures were well rehearsed; Walpole saw to that. On a given day—he would never say which—he would set a little field at Tilden Park's South Gate on fire. "He would radio in," reports early park worker Joe Williams, "saying there was a 929 at South Gate. He would stand right there and watch everybody fight this fire. Afterwards he would double check all the equipment and talk about whatever problems we'd had putting out the fire. Then we were ready for whatever the season would bring.

"And every year, he would light up the same field," concludes Williams. Nobody ever

got lost going to Walpole's fire drills.

But most of the time fighting fires was no picnic. "We used to start on the fire lines at about two in the afternoon," remembers Dick Mauler, another early park worker, "and many times we were on fires all that afternoon and probably most of the night. We never had any routine means of getting food, and we'd get it from the strangest places. All of a sudden the Salvation Army would show up out of nowhere with the canteen truck.

"I remember one time we were at Anthony Chabot on a fire all night, and we were nearly freezing to death because of the fog. All of us from the fire line pooled our resources. I think we had about $2 among us. We sent some-

body down to Oakland to see if he could at least get us a dozen doughnuts to carry us through the night.

"We all looked like we were in pretty bad shape after fighting the fire all night, and so I guess they took pity on him. Somebody down in Oakland felt so sorry they sent up 15 or 20 dozen doughnuts.

"It was really heartwarming. Members of the local community would show up with an ice chest full of beer or canned drinks. Several times some of the families that lived in the park homes would get together and make up sandwiches and send them out to us. But we didn't have any set organization, and so you never knew, when you went out to a fire, when you'd eat again."

Trail safety also got an early start with a horseman—the District's version of "mounted police"—who patrolled the trails from Tilden to Redwood for years. "He and his horse were both pretty old," remembers Collins. Another early ranger guarded the golf course.

The public safety program grew with the increasing park usage. Those early rangers—gruff, hard-bitten former police officers—were replaced by younger men of a different character, and the horse gave way to a green sedan with red light and siren.

The rangers' official uniform began with Ron Day, the District's first full-time peace officer, who bought himself first a badge, then a pair of green pants, a leather belt with a holster, and—in a last-ditch attempt to look official—a pair of old army lieutenant's bars, which he put on upside down. Little by little he built up the uniform and a new Department of Public Safety.

Public Safety Officer Ron Day, who unofficially developed the ranger uniform, wears the uniform as it had evolved by the early 1960s.

A Successful Two Decades

By its 20th birthday in 1954, the District had a budget of $652,000 supporting 5,400 acres of parklands, with 47 full-

---

NIMITZ WAY

Just off Inspiration Point in Tilden Park is a two-mile scenic road with vistas overlooking the Golden Gate, the San Pablo Reservoir, and surrounding valleys. Blooming wild flowers abound there, planted by Fleet Admiral Chester W. Nimitz, the "Johnny Appleseed of Tilden Park." Hiking that road, Admiral Nimitz used to scatter seeds, often of the yellow lupine, one of his favorites.

Robert Sibley, President of the Board of Directors, himself an enthusiastic hiker, encountered the former Chief of Naval Operations so frequently that he felt the roadway should be renamed Nimitz Way.

At the dedication of Nimitz Way, a hiking trail in Tilden Park, Admiral Chester W. Nimitz, left, and Director Robert Sibley, right, inspect the monument marking the start of the trail.

And so it was, on May 5, 1955. Ribbon-cutting ceremonies included over 300 civic and military dignitaries and were followed by tea at the Brazil Building, where Mrs. Nimitz, a noted artist, hung some of her watercolors of the park.

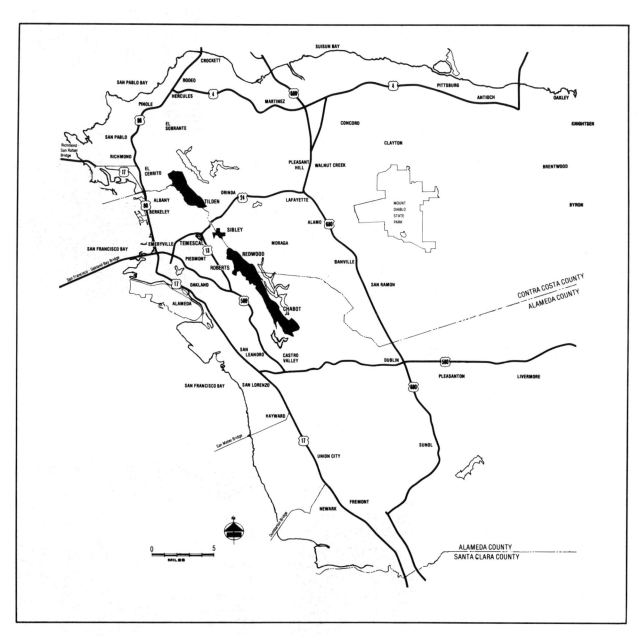

Map shows District parklands in 1960, at the end of the era of General Manager Richard Walpole.

time and 43 seasonal and part-time employees hosting 2.7 million visitors: a record worth celebrating.

With careful management of District resources, General Manager Walpole was able to amass a comfortable surplus with an eye toward future land acquisition. When poor health forced him to resign in 1960, he could look back with pride on having nurtured the District through a period of careful growth and solid development of recreational facilities.

3

William Penn Mott and the Quantum Leap Forward

T he 1960s, as it turned out, would be a revolutionary decade—for the country and for the Park District. Roused from the complacency of the 1950s, the nation explored the New Frontier of President John F. Kennedy, warred on poverty under President Lyndon B. Johnson's Great Society program, and by the end of the decade appeared to be in the midst of a full-scale cultural turnaround. It was a time of dramatic growth in technology as well as management techniques, in urbanization as well as conservation issues.

The District moved in step with these changing times, pausing only momentarily to search for a new General Manager, while Wesley Adams stepped in temporarily to fill the top slot.

"An Idea a Minute!"

The quantum leap forward began in 1962 with the arrival of William Penn Mott, Jr., former Oakland Superintendent of Parks, as General Manager. Combining creative management, a flair for enlisting public support, and "an idea a minute," Bill Mott initiated a whirlwind of expansion that began the spread of regional parks throughout the East Bay.

Ensuring a solid base from which to launch his program required several steps: more skilled professionals to head the departments, a more stable financial base, and better planning for land acquisition and development.

47

For a start, Mott reorganized the administrative functions. Anticipating the District's long-range growth, he developed separate departments for finance, planning, acquisition, equipment, interpretation, park operations, and public relations, and he sought skilled experts to head them. Bob Herman was hired as Controller, Irwin Luckman as head of Plans, Design, and Construction, and Perry Laird as Chief of Parks. Dick Trudeau was brought in to head up the expanded public relations program, Hulet Hornbeck to fill the newly created position of Chief of Land Acquisition, and Chris Nelson to develop a contemporary broad-scale education and interpretation program. Bob Clark was in charge of the Equipment and Fire Operations. The new headquarters building on Skyline Boulevard, which was completed in 1962, provided space for these experts and headquarters staffs.

Mott's enthusiastic vision of a grand scheme of hilltop and shoreline parks required additional and stable funding to back it up, and he moved accordingly to enlarge District revenues.

Contra Costa County Joins the District

The first move was to broaden the tax base by persuading Contra Costa County to return to the fold it had left back in 1934. Then the county had been largely rural, and it began to develop as a residential area only after World War II. Returning veterans settled in the central part of the county, raising children rather than crops, and interest in recreation areas sprouted as an outgrowth of this change. But several desultory attempts by Contra Costa County to pass bond acts for parks failed.

Several Contra Costa leaders, among them Robert Kahn, son and nephew of the founders of the Kahn Foundation and a member of the county's Grand Jury, viewed the county's shortage of parks with growing concern, and in 1963 launched a drive to annex most of the county to the East Bay Regional Park District. One small area—the Liberty Union High School District at the eastern end of the county—was not included because asparagus farmers there strongly opposed annexation.

"Not a single picnic table available in Contra Costa County," became the rallying cry of the new pro-annexation group, Citizens for Regional Parks NOW, which was headed by Mayor Lenard Grote of Pleasant Hill. Dr. and Mrs. Clark Kerr (he was President of the University of California) were honorary co-chairmen, and the group included many who would remain active supporters of the District for years af-

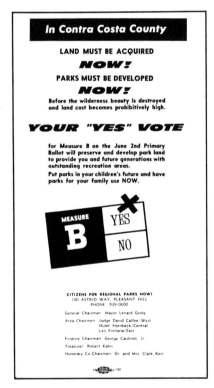

The Citizens for Regional Parks NOW! distributed pamphlets emphasizing the necessity for county park development to persuade citizens of Contra Costa County to vote "Yes" on the 1964 measure to annex to the Park District.

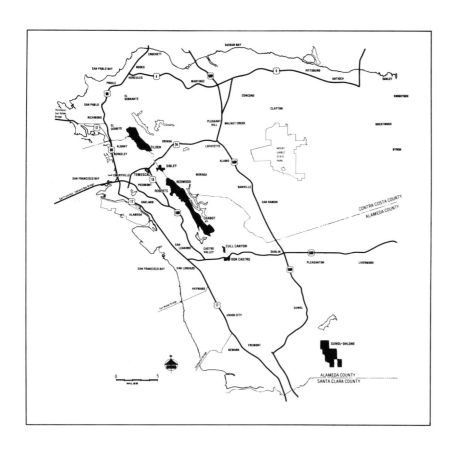

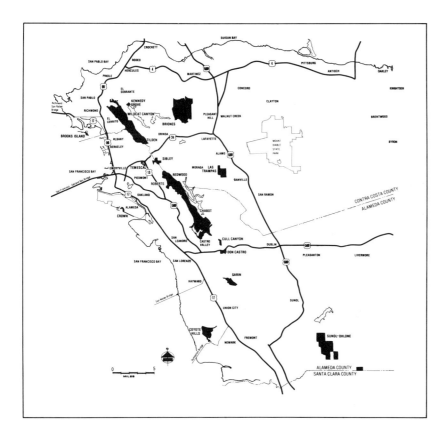

Map above pictures the District as it existed when William Penn Mott, Jr. became General Manager in 1962. Below, 1967 map indicates results of Mott's aggressive policy of park acquisition and development.

49

WILLIAM PENN MOTT, JR.

"He makes things possible that wouldn't happen otherwise." That tribute to William Penn Mott, Jr. by Richard Trudeau, present General Manager, goes a long way toward explaining the explosive growth of the East Bay Regional Park District in the 1960s.

"Because he had such a great belief in what he was doing himself," Trudeau continues, "he had the ability to inspire others to do more and to do better work than they would otherwise."

Mott projected his own immense vitality into the Park District during the years 1962–1967 when he was its General Manager, and left a heritage of open space and recreation for Bay Area residents unmatched anywhere in the country.

His career began in 1933 when the National Park Service hired him as a landscape architect to develop master plans for Death Valley, Sequoia/Kings Canyon, Crater Lake, and Lassen parks.

His executive ability led him into private practice, where he remained until 1942, when Oakland tapped him to become Superintendent of Parks. Garnering private support from citizens and local organizations, he redesigned parks and added such attractions as the Children's Fairyland and the Nature Center at Lake Merritt.

Mott's strong belief that park management required creativity, a more business-like approach, and a surge of citizen participation made him the unanimous choice of the EBRPD Board of Directors when they sought to fill the post of General Manager in 1962.

"Bill Mott turned the whole thing around when he came," asserts then-Director Clyde Woolridge, who helped Director Robert Gordon Sproul persuade Mott to join the District. "Before that we were just coasting along. Bill was the one who went on an aggressive program of enlarging the parks."

He demonstrated early his talents for fund raising, organization, and planning—all needed for the practical application of his goals for the District: financial stability and growth of the parks and their facilities.

Because he believed strongly in providing parks for the people, he also believed in people providing for the parks, and he solicited an average of $100,000 a year in private contributions during his tenure. "We all realized," declares Trudeau, "that Bill was a truly great leader in the field, that he had an ability to bring people along with him who wouldn't have come otherwise."

He brought new life to every aspect of the District's operations, restructuring, reorganizing, bringing in new people, and inspiring the ones who were there. "Bill was a great expansionist, and he had very forward-looking ideas about the development of the Park District," recalls former Direc-

tor Marlin Haley. "He was a fine administrator and a fine gentlemen."

Although the District was growing rapidly, Mott knew every employee by name. Park workers testify that he often stopped on his round of the parks to ask about their families and compliment them on their work. "You'd be at the bottom of a hole digging," recalls one employee, "and you'd look up and see Bill standing there saying, 'How's your mother?' "

His enormous contributions toward beautifying the East Bay were backed up by attention to small details—such as stopping to pick up litter as he walked along. Keeping the parks clean was as necessary as acquiring new ones.

Mott envisioned a ring of parks encircling San Francisco Bay with a system of connecting trails. That dream has not yet come true, but while he was General Manager of the East Bay Regional Park District, Mott made a grand start.

terward. Assemblyman John T. Knox urged a pro vote because "The East Bay Regional Park District is a going concern which has already proved its effectiveness." Hulet Hornbeck, prior to joining the Park District staff, played a major role as Chairman of the Central Contra Costa Committee, as did George Cardinet, who acted as Finance Chairman for the campaign committee. Senator John A. Nejedly, County Counsel at the time, wrote an opinion approving the legality of the proposed action and used his powers of persuasion on the Board of Supervisors.

Annexation was strongly opposed, however, by the county's agricultural interests. With the election date looming, Mott took immediate action to breathe fire into the campaign. He himself went on a day-and-night speaking circuit—"PTAs, Boy Scouts, Rotary Club, Kiwanis, Lions, everything"—and threw the job of running the annexation campaign to Dick Trudeau. "You don't even have to show up at the office," Mott told Trudeau. "Just get the situation organized."

Together Trudeau and Mott crisscrossed the county negotiating with city officials, while at the same time, Trudeau organized support committees and launched a strategic campaign of media coverage. Particularly effective were his feature stories that ran in the sports section of the local newspapers where they were sure to be seen.

Their efforts were victorious, although the margin was narrow: 54 percent in favor, 46 percent against. Eighteen years later, in 1981, the remaining pocket of Contra Costa outside the District, now considerably larger in population, was annexed.

"The citizens groups who got behind us made the difference," asserts Mott. "In fact, I don't think we could have done it without them."

In turn, the citizens would benefit enormously, because the District would use the increased tax monies immediately to develop Kennedy Grove and Briones Regional Park, two areas where the county had acquired land but did not have funds for improvements, and to begin in earnest a major expansion program in Contra Costa County.

A Firm Financial Base

The tax base was further broadened in '66 when Pleasanton annexed to the District by an overwhelming affirmative vote of 80 percent. Now the District had regional park responsibilities in an area of 1,000 square miles serving 1.7 million people.

Increasing the tax base with the annexations helped, but

that alone would not ensure financial stability. More people to serve meant more parks, more equipment, and more personnel. Mott strongly advocated buying land ahead of the real estate developers, and for this the District needed increased tax revenues. The state legislators agreed, and in 1963 they passed a bill for a temporary five-cent tax override, limiting use of the funds to acquisition and capital improvements. In 1967 these limitations were removed, and in 1971 the override became permanent.

The new influx of funds would not have been possible without citizen participation. "People from various organizations not only helped to get the tax bills passed," asserts Mott, "but they also provided funding: the Boy Scouts, the Girl Scouts, and the YMCA all helped fund projects such as the camps we developed."

A firm financial base was now assured, and Mott could turn his attention to the parks themselves.

Kennedy Grove Regional Recreation Area

County-owned lands that became Kennedy Grove Regional Recreational Area and Briones Regional Park were deeded to the District following the annexation, but the District had to start from scratch in developing them. Kennedy Grove was soon transformed into a lush, eucalyptus-wooded area

Groups can reserve picnic areas in Kennedy Grove for barbeques in a sylvan setting.

offering barbeque pits for picnicking, hiking, a turfed play area, horseshoe pits, and a volleyball court.

It was the first park to be opened fully complete and ready to go, but its heavy use soon caused problems of traffic congestion in the nearby residential neighborhood. The District, intent on preserving community peace, hit on a creative solution: park use was restricted to organizations and large groups with advance reservations. In 1982 funding finally became available for an access road, and in 1983 the park was once again open for general public use.

Meanwhile, at Briones, where the Bear Creek watershed and ridges offered scenic terrain for hiking, horseback riding, and picnicking, the District needed to construct only a few facilities before opening the park to the public in 1967. At the dedication ceremonies, State Senator John Nejedly received a national award for conservation efforts; he had been particularly helpful in the Briones acquisition.

Las Trampas Regional Wilderness

Further park development in Contra Costa County was spurred by the timely passage of a 1964 state bond issue, which provided money to counties and their local jurisdictions for parkland development. The District used its share of funds designated for parks in Contra Costa County to acquire Las Trampas Regional Wilderness. With additional help from federal grants, the Las Trampas parklands were gradually extended, so that today the park offers visitors 3,270 acres of unspoiled wilderness with breathtaking views in all directions. In 1976 the District acquired a private picnic facility nearby, the Little Hills Ranch Regional Recreation Area, which offers facilities for picnics, swimming, and other group activities on a reservable basis.

Cooperation between county, state, and federal governments and the District which made Las Trampas Wilderness possible was fast becoming a full-blown art, and the District today has a long record of parks acquired by unique cooperative arrangements with government agencies at all levels.

Coyote Hills Regional Park

At the same time that Las Trampas was being acquired with 1964 state bond money, the District earmarked much of its Alameda County bond act funds for Coyote Hills Regional Park. Acquiring the land—which ultimately involved condemnation proceedings—required all the delicate negotiating skills the District could muster. Hulet Hornbeck's gentle, straightforward approach ensured that the former landown-

Aerial view of Coyote Hills Regional Park near Fremont where visitors can find a self-guiding nature trail, board-walks for viewing freshwater marshes, interpretive center, and guided tours of the Indian shell mounds and reconstructed Indian village.

53

SEALS IN THE HILLS?

The Park District often inherited long-standing problems—such as the eroding sand at Crown Beach—when it acquired a park, but at Coyote Hills the territory came with an unusual and thoroughly entertaining attraction.

Dr. Thomas C. Poulter, Director of Stanford Research Institute's Biological Sonar Laboratory located at Coyote Hills, was studying seals, sea lions, and river otters to discover what their physiology might reveal about human obesity, the aging process, multiple sclerosis, and fatal shock. Knowledge of the highly sophisticated sonar system by which these animals navigate in darkness and unerringly find food might aid the human blind. Dr. Poulter also experimented with methods of human communication with the seals.

The District realized the value of such work as an interpretive program, and arranged with Dr. Poulter to hold open houses for the public after the park was opened. Soon groups were touring the laboratory regularly—including school classes ranging from kindergarten to the college level—viewing the California and Stellar sea lions, the

Gray, Harbor, Fur, Harp, and Elephant seals, and the river otters.

Dr. Poulter, a distinguished scientist who had served as second in command on Admiral Richard E. Byrd's second Antarctic expedition in 1933–35 and held two special congressional medals awarded in 1940 and 1947, believed the public should become more acquainted with the scientific experiments carried on in the lab. "Man has discovered a system that the sea lion has been using for millions of years and has developed to a

much higher degree than our most effective electronic instruments," said Dr. Poulter at the time.

This unusual interpretive program was enjoyed by the public for nearly five years, but the research carried on by Dr. Poulter ultimately came to an end, and the laboratory was closed. Today all that remain of seals in the hills are photographs and memories of an unusually talented scientist and his contribution to the District.

ers remained friends of the District. "I never consider any acquisition as an adversary relationship with any property owner," maintains Hornbeck, emphasizing a District philosophy which remains a hallmark to this day.

With a 23,000-acre wildlife refuge as its neighbor, Coyote Hills has become an educational park, preserving and interpreting valuable marshland wildlife and 2,300-year-old Indian shell mounds.

Sunol Regional Wilderness

Balancing this educational park in southern Alameda County was Sunol, a Regional Wilderness Park. It was purchased in 1962, although negotiations—as was usually the case—had been under way for several years. Former Board Director Clyde Woolridge, who joined the Board in 1958, found himself in the midst of discussions about Sunol. He recalls the problem that sometimes plagued the District in land acquisitions. "The price was reasonable, although it was only 'goat country,' as someone called it then." But when the local press headlined the District's interest, the price jumped 15 percent, and that was what the District had to pay.

As a wilderness, Sunol features overnight family camping and backpacking, interpretive programs, picnicking, birdwatching, and trails for hiking, jogging, and horseback riding.

When more property was added in the years 1965-1969, youth groups could hike up the creek six miles to Camp Ohlone, a delightful, secluded wilderness camping spot. The creek has water in it all year round, clear enough for swimming. Farther east is the new, yet to be opened, 5,776-acre Ohlone Regional Wilderness.

At Camp Ohlone there are 260 acres of wilderness suitable for camping and backpacking on a reservation basis only. Here also District naturalists host a "Week of Wilderness" science education camp for children ages 11–15.

Scenic Lanes Provide a Climatic Assist

District parks now dotted the East Bay ridges from Kennedy Grove in the north to Sunol in the south. Presenting a variety of activities, these hill parks—Olmsted's "scenic lanes"—also had a beneficial impact on the area's climate by leaving the greenery in place. This allowed for the removal of the carbon dioxide from the air, the evaporation of moisture, and the recycling of the fog vapor, keeping the trees green and the air clear.

The District was quickly becoming more aware of its important role in maintaining the delicate ecological balance in an increasingly urban and industrial area. "It's similar to the situation when we filled the Bay," remarks Robert Kahn, longtime District advocate. "At first we didn't know what would happen when we reduced the surface area of the Bay and eliminated the marshlands, which were easiest to fill but where the water was oxygenated. But we soon found out when the fish died."

This distressing development spurred the formation of an organization dedicated to reversing the trend: the Save San Francisco Bay Association.

"People Want To Get To The Water"

Save the Bay was the brainchild of Kay Kerr, wife of the President of the University of California and longtime East Bay resident. Alarmed by a study that reported the Bay was being filled at a rate of 3.6 square miles per year and would be a river by the year 2020, she mobilized a small but determined committee to lobby for an end to uncontrolled filling.

In 1963, the Save San Francisco Bay Association obtained money for a study which eventually led to the formation by the state legislature of the San Francisco Bay Conservation and Development Commission (BCDC) with authority over all filling of the Bay. The Park District joined energetically in this grass roots campaign to preserve the Bay, the success of which set off a chain reaction against destruction of wetlands and unwise filling of bays and rivers.

The Save the Bay campaign reinforced a growing concern on the part of the District to acquire shoreline parks. Bill Mott had served a term as President of the Association, and he was well aware of the need for public parks along the Bayshore. "There were a limited number of places where you had access to the Bay," Mott explains, "and with the intensive programs for filling in the Bay for industrial development, I felt that the Regional Park District needed to think about acquiring more than just ridgetop lands."

"It was done," continues Trudeau, "with what you could call malice aforethought, because we knew that that would mean a better quality of life for people living in the District. People want to get to the water." Shoreline parks would also bring open spaces closer to the people who lived in the inner city and had little access to the hilltops.

Crown Memorial State Beach

Alameda State Beach presented the first opportunity for a shoreline park, but fraught with problems, it proved to be something of an albatross weighing heavily on the District for the next 15 or so years.

The beach's colorful history dates back to the 1880s when it first became a resort area. In its 1917–1939 heyday as Neptune Beach, it featured an amusement park with vast swimming pools and carnival rides, making it the "Coney Island of the West."

The property was acquired in 1942 by the War Shipping Board and used for training future ships' officers, and in

1957 Assemblyman Robert Crown successfully campaigned to have the state acquire it for a swimming beach.

Meanwhile, marshes and mudflats along the southern Alameda shoreline were filled in by Utah Construction and Mining Company to create an area for residential and commercial buildings. An artificial beach was constructed along the south shore, and it has been eroding almost ever since. The fine-grain sand kept slipping away, and no combination of remedies tried for the next two decades succeeded in keeping the sand in its proper place. The city of Alameda, which had assumed responsibility for this southern part of the beach, turned its management over to the Park District in 1967. At the same time the District acquired responsibility for the state-owned beach, and in 1974 named the entire shoreline area the Robert W. Crown Memorial State Beach in honor of the assemblyman who worked hard for its preservation.

For the next twelve years, the District grappled—sometimes to the point of despair—with the thorny problem of erosion, which by the late 1970s was so serious that it had begun to expose electrical lines and undermine Shoreline Drive.

Neptune Beach was a popular local beach and amusement park, an Alameda landmark from 1917 to 1939, located at what is now Crown Memorial State Beach. Its carnival rides included the aptly named "Whoopee" roller coaster. Other attractions included two large swimming pools, an 8,000-seat stadium for baseball, football, and motorcycle or midget auto races, private picnic groves, a ballroom, and a cafeteria.

Crown Beach offers scenic vistas across the Bay.

With the help of the U.S. Army Corps of Engineers, which in the late 1970s tested 18 different low-cost techniques for erosion control, and the city of Alameda, which joined forces with the District to seek immediate remedies, the District finally settled on an innovative plan of heavy sand with groins and sandtraps to confine the sand to the beach area. (Groins are sheet piles reinforced with concrete.)

Funding for such a mammoth project totaling $2.5 million came from the State Energy and Resources Fund, authorized in the state's 1981 and 1982 budgets, the city of Alameda, and the District, whose allocation was obtained by the untiring efforts of State Assemblymen Elihu Harris and Nicholas Petris. But Operation Sandpour, as the project came to be known, was not yet out of the woods. During the 1981 and 1982 budget hearings, project funding was threatened by a myriad of technical and financial questions and doubts posed by the Legislative Analyst and the legislators. Only numerous trips to Sacramento and persistent lobbying by the District succeeded in overcoming these hurdles, and in early 1982 more than 200,000 cubic yards of medium grade sand were dredged from the bottom of San Francisco Bay between Alcatraz and Angel Island, barged to Alameda, and pumped directly onto the beach through a 7,000-foot, 18-inch diameter plastic pipe. Tested by the severe storms of the spring and winter of 1982, the beach has held firm. "It is the only successful West Coast project of its kind," General Manager Trudeau proudly observes.

Rededicated in September 1982, it is the largest and most heavily used swimming beach on San Francisco Bay. With its open, grassy spots, a long, narrow strip of sand, and a gentle slope extending into the water for some distance, it forms a pleasant and safe place for wading and swimming and offers wide vistas across the Bay.

In the next decade, the District added several more shoreline parks, until at present, District parks dot the 150-mile shoreline between Antioch and Fremont. Acquiring and developing them presented a special challenge, since much of the shoreline was already industrialized, but these parks are some of the most beautiful and most visited in the system.

Recreation: Another Mott Objective

While land acquisition thus escalated along both the ridges and the shoreline, recreational development of existing parks skyrocketed.

Mott believed wholeheartedly in family amusements, and

EQUIPMENT, MORE OR LESS

General Manager William Penn Mott's guiding principle, as he implemented his creative plans for District growth, was that progress required both productive people and proper tools. He quickly attended to both those needs.

At that time, most of the District's equipment was 10- or 15-year old World War II surplus. Assistant General Manager Jerry Kent tells this story he heard from park workers: "After that big flood in October of '62, Mott came down South Park Drive in Tilden Park and found a group of people with shovels trying to clear the debris from a landslide. He asked them where the District backhoe was— which would have made their job a whole lot easier—and they told him they didn't have one. So he just went out and got a backhoe and started it working. As I understand it, the District had never used a backhoe before and didn't have any equipment to do that kind of major slide repair."

Sometimes, instead of buying new equipment, they revitalized what they had.

"We had an old World War II surplus boom flatbed truck with winches on it," continues Kent, "but we didn't have any cranes or any large boom equipment. My father was in trailer manufacturing, and I knew how to weld; so I offered to build a boom truck. I took a large, one-ton flatbed truck, and then welded a crane structure on the back. I did it all at the old Tilden Park corporation yard, and it took about three weeks."

With new equipment and ingenious renovations of the war surplus machinery, the District was able to provide its people with the tools necessary to implement Mott's plans.

Cull Canyon as it appeared in 1964. The water level at the award-winning swimming lagoon is maintained by pumping water from the reservoir (left) into the inner lagoon (right). Today, after extensive landscaping, the area is lush with trees.

he pursued the development of recreational attractions in his characteristically energetic and enthusiastic manner. Announcing to his periodic gathering of employees that the Park District was going to be the greatest in the country, he launched a vigorous program to improve the quality and quantity of equipment, and to renovate old buildings and construct new ones.

Swimming Lagoons: A Prize-winning Concept

Renovations included dredging Lake Temescal and rebuilding both Lake Anza and Temescal beaches. New development included the swimming lagoons at Cull Canyon and Don Castro in the southern part of the District. They were reservoirs formed by Alameda County Flood Control District dams and leased to the Park District. At Cull Canyon there was boating and fishing, and, in an innovative move, a secondary dam was built to provide an inner swimming area complete with sandy beach.

The idea of an inner swimming lagoon had never been

HAULING OLIVE TREES

Shortcuts can sometimes end up being the long way around, as the District discovered when they decided to landscape the just-completed swim lagoon at Cull Canyon with a grove of large, mature olive trees.

Ordinarily, the appropriate requisition order would have been filed, with all the attendant bureaucratic delays, but Chief of Parks Perry Laird knew how to get some trees fast, from a friend who had an olive grove in Sacramento. Jerry Kent, then Superintendent of Maintenance, was dispatched with a crew of four or five men, a flatbed truck, a large transport truck, and a backhoe. "We had never dug up olive trees before in our lives, didn't have the slightest idea of what we were doing," confesses Kent, "but that's what we were told to do.

"In Sacramento, we dug the trees and loaded them onto the trucks. That was fine. Then we started back toward the Bay Area, and that's when the trouble began. First we were stopped at Davis by the Highway Patrol because the

loads of trees were too wide, and they were too high to go under the overpasses. Then, it turned out we didn't have a permit for a wide load. Those trees were in violation of every law there was."

One of the crew was dispatched to Oakland where he waded through official red tape in record time to obtain the permit. "And we had to stay overnight by the side of the road at Davis," Kent continues, "while we waited for the permit."

Meanwhile, the crew was faced with the task of keeping the trees from wilting in the withering central valley heat. "We had to go into town and bring back water to spray on the trees to keep them alive," recalls Kent. "We stayed up all night watering those trees, but they all lived. We finally got them to Cull Canyon, and they were planted in time for the dedication, but that whole adventure was hardly the shortcut we thought it would be."

tried before. Irwin Luckman, head of the Plans and Designs Department, designed it to provide year-round, silt-free swimming. When the water level fell as the summer wore on, water could be pumped out of the reservoir into the inner lagoon. It was an immediate hit, and when Mott took a count of swimmers, he found that there were usually ten times as many people at Cull as at nearby swimming pools.

The lagoon was also an artistic triumph, winning the 1966 Governor's Design Award for Exceptional Distinction for Recreational Development in the category of Landscape.

Don Castro Regional Recreational Area offers both scenic beauty for hiking and fishing and group activities at the swimming lagoon and picnic areas.

Chabot Equestrian Center and the swim complex at Lake Anza were also a part of this award.

When the Flood Control District created the Don Castro Reservoir, the Park District constructed a similar lagoon there.

Lake Chabot

Meanwhile, negotiations were under way with EBMUD during the early '60s which would allow—for the first time—public use of one of its water storage reservoirs, Lake Chabot, which adjoined Anthony Chabot Regional Park (formerly Grass Valley). The initial lease agreement in 1964 called

Lake Chabot offers visitors peace and tranquility.

for boating and fishing on the lake, with hiking and camping in the surrounding forest.

On the leased riparian willow land at the upper end of the lake, Mott arranged to have a private concessionaire build the Willow Park Golf Course. Before construction could begin, however, the original concessionaire went broke, and a new group of investors had to be found to complete the project. Finally, the 18-hole course and clubhouse opened in 1966.

A Turning Point

Then a group of citizens concerned about the propriety of the new golf concession requested California State Assemblyman John T. Knox, Chairman of the Assembly Local Government Committee and a potent force in the legislature, to look into the matter.

Knox's two-day hearings presented the District with one of its greatest challenges thus far. What might have turned into a Pandora's-box probe of all the District's problems became instead a thoughtful inquiry into mistakes in the handling of the golf course construction. Thanks to the efforts of then-Director of Public Information Dick Trudeau, over 100 people wrote letters or appeared at the hearings to testify in favor of the Park District, an overwhelming display of public approval that totally engulfed the opposition.

As a result of the hearings, Assemblyman Knox became one of the District's staunchest supporters. And as one of California's most potent legislators, he spent his remaining terms vigorously supporting and protecting parklands in the East Bay.

The hearings and the seemingly interminable legal problems over the Willow Park course had little effect on golfers

THE OPENING OF LAKE CHABOT

Park openings were always occasions for festive celebration, but at the Lake Chabot opening in 1966 the crowd's enthusiasm almost spoiled the show.

It was a particularly rewarding day for the District staff and the Board of Directors, because people had been waiting for years for the opportunity to fish in the lake. The crowd's impatience became apparent early in the day, when thousands of fidgeting fishermen lined up on the road that runs along the west side of the lake, poles at the ready, waiting for the starting whistle to blow. One overanxious angler could not resist taking just a practice cast—and immediately landed a two-pound bass. This set off instant bedlam, as the rest of the crowd, heedless that the whistle still had not blown, eagerly cast their lines.

When order was restored, the traditional prayer for the safety and success of the fisherman was said, a mariachi band serenaded the anglers, and the fishing derby was ready to go.

That first day of fishing and fun became standard fare at Lake Chabot, and it is ceremoniously repeated once a year at the annual fishing derby.

in the south county, who were happy enough to tee off close to home. Other special interest groups also found their place in the parks. Horsemen, for example, wanted to practice riding for the hunt, and to accommodate them, the District built a hunt field in Redwood Park. No one was quite sure how to build the jumps, however, and construction crews had to rebuild some of them several times before they got them right.

Expansion on All Fronts

With the prolific spread of new parks and new facilities, the District sometimes resorted to "crisis management" to meet the crunch of deadlines for park openings, with crews working around the clock to finish a job.

Fortunately, Mott believed in professional equipment as well as professional people. Soon after he took command, he launched a program to acquire more up-to-date trucks, earth moving machines, scoopmobiles, tractors, and horticultural tools. By the mid-'60s, the District had state-of-the-art equipment equaling that of any park agency in California.

The dramatic expansion on all fronts of the District's activities renewed interest and concern among citizens of the two counties. The number of Board members had jumped

---

CRISIS MANAGEMENT

"Crisis Management" is the name park employees give to a style developed during the 1960s when parks were opening like poppies in a spring meadow.

Take Cull Canyon, for example. The District had announced six months earlier that Cull Canyon would be opening on a certain date—opening ceremonies required at least that much lead time. As the date approached and the park was still not completed, construction crews quickly had to assemble extra men and materials to meet the deadline. By pulling crews from every park, they managed to finish the work in record time, so that the park was ready for the dedication. But when that deadline crunch was met, others immediately loomed.

"When we did the Tee Club," remembers carpenter/locksmith Bud Scott, "we had a man per square foot there. You would no sooner put a piece of wood on the wall when a painter would come along and paint it."

"If you hung sheetrock," adds carpenter Truman Rhoades, "they would be right behind to tape it. On the Moraga Trail, we had three weeks. We finished that trail one day before the third week was up, and they had a big dedication for the Fourth of July. And they had a picnic for us when we finished it."

"We still have the deadline crunch today," remarks Park Supervisor Jim Howland, somewhat wryly. "But miraculously, the work always seems to get done."

"Sure," adds Horticultural Specialist Grady Simril. "When you work 48 hours a day, you can do it."

The Botanic Garden at Tilden is divided into various ecological areas of California, each displaying its native plants. Here the Alpine Meadow depicts a grassy meadow in the high Sierras.

DR. ROBERT GORDON SPROUL

Dr. Robert Gordon Sproul, President Emeritus of the University of California, served as a distinguished member of the Board of Directors from 1958 to 1967, becoming its President in 1964.

One of the District's founding fathers in 1934, he carried on their dreams of environmental preservation as he helped guide the District through its later periods of growth. When he persuaded William Penn Mott, Jr. to take the position of General Manager of the Park District in 1962, Dr. Sproul acted as catalyst for the dramatic growth of the parks in the 1960s.

Mott himself pays tribute to the Board President's leadership: "President Sproul was particularly effective with the state legislature, because he knew those people and he had a tremendous reputation up and down the state. He was just a marvelous person. It was a great thrill to work with him."

Dr. Sproul summed up his work with the Park District in a message contained in *The Story of a Nickel* written in 1965: "Since its creation more than thirty years ago, the members of the Board of Directors and the management and staff of the District have endeavored to follow the credo of Daniel Burnham: 'Make no little plans. Aim high.' We have made no little plans, nor have our aceomplishments been small."

"Old Betsy," on the left, was retired in 1966 after cutting more than 60,000 miles of grass at the Tilden Park golf course. Standing in front are Fred Uchishiba (left) and Antonio Reyes. Seated on "Young Jake," the new gang mower, is Lawrence McDonald.

from five to seven when Contra Costa County was annexed, with two representing only Contra Costa County wards, two representing only Alameda County wards, and three representing two-county areas. More and more people showed up at Board meetings, and the press began covering the meetings in local newspapers.

Sometimes the issues were quite hot: the Botanic Garden was one. Under the diligent supervision of James Roof for many years, it was scheduled for removal to Chabot, where it would be considerably enlarged. Devotees of native plants, however, organizing themselves under the banner of The Friends of the Botanic Garden, protested that some of the more fragile plants would never survive the transplanting. The Directors bowed to their wishes and left the Garden intact in Tilden Park under James Roof's care.

Campaigns such as this one reflected the growing public awareness of the parks and their value, not only for recreation but for conservation and preservation of indigenous plants and open space as well.

Interpretation: "One of the Great Assets"

Some of this awareness was the outgrowth of the District's earliest educational work, launched by Jack Parker shortly after World War II. His Junior Rangers and hikers grew up to be voters who helped pass the state bond acts in the '60s and '70s. But it was William Penn Mott, Jr., arriving as General Manager in the '60s, who significantly spurred the growth of the interpretive function of the District.

"We set up an interpretive division with Chris Nelson in charge," recalls Mott, "and I think that that's become one of the great assets of the Regional Park District. One of the big reasons why people are so supportive of the District is because they have this outstanding interpretive department. And we need this education desperately."

At the time Chris Nelson became head of the newly created interpretive department, the nature study program was housed in old, dilapidated CCC shacks, which were drafty and unheated. Mice ran over the typewriter keys, and old bricks shored up the foundations.

Recalls Nelson of the sizeable task facing him, "Mott wanted the most innovative, creative interpretive program ever devised, and he wanted an innovative, creative interpretive center that would set new standards in programs and exhibition for the park field. That was the charge I was given."

He immediately set out to improve the nature study programs for the schools, surveying their curriculum needs and developing such programs as Indian culture and stream erosion, with hands-on activities rather than lectures. On Saturdays, as part of a natural history program, children might learn to make toys as the pioneer children did. Teaching aides, such as the puppet show "Lester Litterbug Learns His Lessons," which dramatized the litter problem, were produced with the aid of naturalist Josh Barkin and his wife, Pearl, who volunteered their evenings for puppet-making.

Barkin, who had joined the Park District in 1960, was one of the interpretive program's greatest assets. He established a strong rapport with children and had a genius for keeping their rapt attention with such programs as a puppet show on conservation of energy and study tours of gutters and shopping centers to explore the kinds of natural life found in cities.

Because he felt that people had lost sight of where their food came from, he toured the local grocery stores, avid youngsters in tow, pointing out the origins of each item. General Manager Trudeau calls him "the foremost interpretive teacher in our time anywhere in the country," and he was constantly in demand to help train national and state naturalists.

The CCC shack eventually—after eight years of planning and hard work—gave way in 1974 to a striking new Environmental Education Center, which has won accolades from children and architects alike. Its Nocturnal Animal Hall, when complete, will add a new dimension to wildlife study.

General Manager William Penn Mott, Jr. takes a turn at feeding the deer at the Nature Area in Tilden Park. The Nature Area was an important element in the developing interpretative program.

Marshaling Public Support

If interpretation was one of the crucial items on Mott's agenda, public relations was another, two sides of the same coin of reaching out to the public.

Under Dick Trudeau, the concept of bringing the Park District into the public's awareness matured into a full-blown art, requiring not only day-to-day legwork but also anticipation of future demands and challenges.

A good public relations program was essential because, as Mott observes, "People take parks for granted, and when it comes to budget time, parks are always at the bottom of the budget."

Trudeau began with a series of radio and television spots to draw public attention to the District, followed by a blitz of brochures and other materials to highlight specific issues. Like all the members of Mott's team, he threw himself wholeheartedly into every project. When the District needed legislation, Trudeau commuted to Sacramento to confer with legislators. Back home, he marshaled support from city officials, business leaders, the media, park users, and neighbors.

"Of course, you really don't accomplish anything all by yourself," he insists. "You have to have a lot of other people involved with you. You have to inspire other people to work with you: volunteers, people in the community. If you can inspire them by your own example of what you feel and what you do and what it means to you, and you have a sincere belief in what you're doing, that carries over and you can get them to work with you. Then a lot of things are possible that wouldn't be possible otherwise."

He and Mott believed that this sort of dynamic partnership between public agencies and the private sector leads to a better quality of life for everyone, one of the goals that inspired the formation of the District in the '30s.

The growing public awareness and understanding of this unique Park District and the dramatic success of Mott and his staff in revitalizing the District's programs led to increasing local, state, and national visibility; the *New York Times* assigned a reporter to the District, and visitors came from around the world.

The Tilden Park Merry-Go-Round is enjoyed by visitors from around the world, as well as by local families. Here a delegation of officials from Tanzania ends a 1967 tour of the parks with a musical ride.

The End of an Era

In early 1967, the regional park era of Bill Mott formally ended when then-Governor Ronald Reagan persuaded him to become Director of California's Department of Parks and Recreation. Irwin Luckman served as General Manager in

1967, and following his resignation in 1968, Dick Trudeau was named Acting General Manager. The next year, the Board, after an extensive nationwide search, appointed Trudeau to the post permanently.

Trudeau inherited a greatly expanded District. From its modest size of 10,500 acres in 1962, it had now grown to 20 parks totaling 22,000 acres, serving two counties with a population of over 1.5 million. The total budget approached $12 million, and visitors had more than tripled.

Challenges abounded. Urbanization was occurring at an alarming rate; the population projected for the year 2000 was 3.1 million. Booming land development and housing construction, plus steady inflation, would require the District to move fast and effectively to preserve open space at an affordable price. The agency would need to rely heavily on the management skills it had honed over the past decade: long-range planning, fiscal accountability, professional expertise in public relations, interpretation, design, acquisition and development, plus the creative cooperation of government, public agencies, and the private sector.

If the past decade had seen the District explode in growth, it was simple preparation for the opportunities of the 1970s.

4
Aiming High: The Challenges of The Trudeau Era

The new decade ushered in new leadership, new sophistication, new financing, new parks, and new crises. Even before the 1970s had begun, the new General Manager, Richard Trudeau, successfully met and resolved his first crisis and turned it to the District's advantage.

The controversy involved Apperson Ridge, which has gone down in District annals as a major turning point.

Lying adjacent to Sunol Regional Wilderness, the Ridge—then agricultural and grazing land—contains basalt and valuable rock, and in 1968 Utah Construction and Mining Company proposed to quarry the entire 1,200-foot ridgetop for rock. Utah obtained a 30-year lease on the property from owner William Apperson and requested a zoning variance from the Alameda County Board of Supervisors. Quarrying operations would not only have brought the ridge down below the level of the surrounding hills, but would also have meant years of trucks, dirt, and noise intruding on the neighboring wilderness park. The District, alert to these threats, immediately filed an objection. Taking advantage of the 1970s' blossoming concern for environmental protection, the General Manager and his staff rallied thousands of conservationists to the fight.

Preferring compromise to outright confrontation, the District offered to withdraw its objections on the condition that Utah agree to a comprehensive list of mitigations including donating other land to the District, but Utah refused. "We put up a great fight and Utah put up a great fight," recalls former Director Paul Harberts, who played a

RICHARD C. TRUDEAU, GENERAL MANAGER

The fact that the size of the District has quadrupled in the last two decades is one tribute to General Manager Richard C. Trudeau, but it hardly says it all. The District has grown because Trudeau has carried forward the vision of the future that characterized its founders.

As a native of Washington state, Dick Trudeau grew up appreciating the values of open space and access to the shoreline. After receiving a Master of Public Administration degree from the Maxwell School of Citizenship and Public Affairs of Syracuse University, he accepted an assignment in Denmark with the United States Department of State. He then went to Seattle, Washington as Regional Director of CARE, and in 1953 was named by *Time* magazine as one of the nation's outstanding newsmakers.

After ten years with the United Crusade, he signed on with the Park District as head of the public relations department. In 1969 the Board named him General Manager.

Particularly concerned with financial stability—the basis for growth—Trudeau has steered an effective course through the legislative mazes on the local, state, and federal level. Working with Assemblyman John Knox and Alameda County Supervisor Joseph Bort, Trudeau lobbied for state legislation for the 1971 tax increase: AB 925. Typically, he began early talking to city and county officials, gathering signatures, arranging for busloads of people to go to the Sacramento hearings. The bill was passed with a carefully crafted compromise, which provided for eight cents of the increase to go for land acquisition and the other two cents for park maintenance and development.

Typical of his can-do spirit are Trudeau's views on the inevitable problem of whether District resources should go for acquisition of new land or for development of existing parks. "You can do both," he states firmly, "but you have to be creative in using the funds that you have to balance one against the other." Such creative funding and utilization of those funds means more parks and facilities for the public's dollar.

Utilization of Trudeau's public relations skills has brought well-deserved national recognition for the District. He has received both the Silver Anvil Award (1963) and the Gold Key Award (1970) from the Public Relations Society of America. Other awards for outstanding leadership and service to parks and recreation through effective administration have come from the National Recreation and Parks Association, the National Association of County Park and Recreation Officials, and the American Society for Public Administration.

In the Park District's 50-year history, there have been leaders of uncommon ability, and Richard Trudeau is carrying that tradition forward to the future.

major role in the struggle himself. "We weren't going to let them affect this park adversely without a quid pro quo for the public."

The District presented a compelling case to the supervisors, emphasizing the investment that had already been made in the park, the value of the wilderness to the quality of East Bay citizens' lives, and the District's unsuccessful

The scenic beauty and tranquility of Sunol Regional Wilderness (pictured above) was threatened in 1968 by an attempt to establish a quarry at Apperson Ridge. Marshaling both public and private support, the District preserved its wilderness, thus establishing itself as a force for environmental protection.

attempts to compromise. After more than a year of public hearings, the supervisors voted four to one against the permit.

The District emerged from this widely publicized contest as a force for changing times, clearly demonstrating its leadership ability in environmental protection. It earned the gratitude of the public and the respect of the state government, both of which would be crucial in the next decade.

Fifteen years later, quarrying on Apperson Ridge would again become an issue, but this time it was the Oliver De Silva Company that sought to establish a quarry.

The scenario could not have been more different. As a developer, Ed De Silva, President of the company, subscribed to the philosophy that development should not remove anything of value to the community without a replacement of equal value, and he had worked closely with the District on several earlier projects.

ACCOMMODATION BENEFITS EVERYONE

The District's ability to avert crisis with compromise and foster public sector/private sector cooperation was never more clearly demonstrated than in its handling of a power line crisis in 1970.

Pacific Gas and Electric Company had long held an easement through Briones Regional Park where it planned to construct a power line. Although the Sierra Club had filed a protest against this trifling with the wilderness, the easement was upheld by the Public Utilities Commission and the State Supreme Court.

Negotiating with both the Sierra Club and PG&E, District General Manager Richard Trudeau proposed that the power lines be shifted from the hilltops to the canyons, a solution that pleased everyone. PG&E saved money, and the District preserved the scenic beauty of the park. Fred Blumberg, then Vice President of the District Board and a member of the negotiating

Hulet Hornbeck, Chief of Land Acquisition, holds map showing the relocation of the power lines in Briones Regional Park at the media conference announcing the agreement between Pacific Gas and Electric Company and the Park District.

team, suggested a final touch: painting the towers an opaque, less metallic color to blend into the landscape.

This peaceful resolution of a thorny issue was announced at an on-the-spot press conference in the middle of Briones Park, with participants flown in by helicopter.

It was another case where the District parlayed a potential confrontation into a plus, and PG&E was so delighted with the results that they later underwrote the kickoff dinner for the District's tax campaign.

The resulting negotiations, which tackled the same issues that had been so troublesome a decade and a half earlier, were intense but amicable, and a Memorandum of Understanding was signed in July 1983. The District withdrew its objections to quarrying, and De Silva, in the precedent-setting mitigation agreement, guaranteed the following: to locate the quarry on the northeastern portion of Apperson Ridge, out of sight and sound of Sunol and Ohlone Regional Wildernesses and most of the Livermore Valley; to limit quarrying to daylight hours and five days a week, with weekends and holidays off; to leave the 2,297-foot ridgeline substantially as it presently exists to prevent climatic changes; to build and maintain a paved access road for the trucks; to regulate blasting; and to protect wildlife and plant life.

In addition, the District would receive from $4.3 million to $8.6 million at current dollar value in economic mitigation over the next 40 years to compensate for unavoidable adverse effects on park users and the two regional wildernesses.

"This story is a remarkable example of how industry and government can work together," remarked Trudeau after the Board signed the agreement.

Contra Loma Helps the Cities

The Apperson Ridge controversy with Utah Construction was a major challenge to the new Trudeau administration, but it was not the only one. Even earlier, in 1968, the General Manager, staff, and the Board of Directors were called upon to help deal with social unrest. That was the year when riots tore through the streets of Pittsburg and threatened Oakland. Part of the problem was lack of recreation opportunities to keep youngsters off the streets, and community officials sent an S.O.S. to the District.

In Oakland, the District began its first busing program in conjunction with the Office of Economic Opportunity, transporting people from the inner city to Roberts and Redwood parks.

Contra Loma Regional Park, opened at first on an emergency basis to help alleviate social unrest in the 60's, now offers a year round sandy beach, fishing, picnicking, boating, trails, and an interpretive program on solar energy.

Pittsburg, however, was too far from any existing District facility to make busing feasible. The District's only possibility was to use land at a nearby reservoir owned by the U.S. Bureau of Reclamation and build a park in record time—a nearly impossible task. Plans for Contra Loma Regional Park were launched immediately.

It meant negotiating an unprecedented interim agreement with the Bureau of Reclamation and then installing all the facilities. "I don't think any public agency anywhere ever moved faster than we did to get Contra Loma open," recalls Trudeau. "We pushed hard, everybody worked together, and we had youngsters on the beach in six weeks."

The District in 1971, shortly after Richard Trudeau was appointed General Manager.

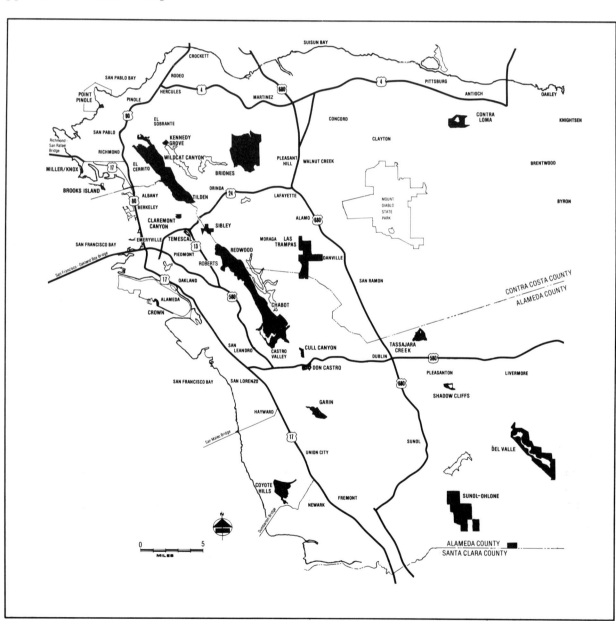

Long-Range Priorities for Acquisition

While resolving these immediate crises, the District also turned its attention to mapping long-range goals for the next decade. Responding to growing public pressure for more parks in southern Alameda County and in Contra Costa County, the Board, in 1970, adopted an aggressive land acquisition priority program. In addition, interest in shoreline parks had been developing since the mid-'60s, and the Board's new program now reaffirmed this shift in emphasis away from hill lands to the shoreline, heretofore largely in private hands.

But it was obvious that such an ambitious program of acquisition along the entire Alameda and Contra Costa shoreline—as well as additional parklands throughout the interior of the District—was impossible without more funds. In a widely circulated public report, the Board advocated a tax increase, arguing that with the funds the District could double the size of the 34 square miles of parks now admin-

---

UNILATERAL OPTIONS

Creative solutions to difficult problems have become a way of life at the Park District. "Nothing works the same way twice," emphasizes General Manager Richard Trudeau. "You have to be flexible and find the solution that fits the situation."

One of those solutions was the brainchild of Jack Rogers, the District's attorney on land matters, and Land Acquisition Chief Hulet Hornbeck, who developed what they called unilateral options. In looking at several parcels of land, Hornbeck would put $100 down on each, making a binding unilateral contract. Getting as many of these as possible, he would then pick the ones that were the best buys, areas where he could gather a number of parcels together. He would get an appraisal on only

those choices, thus saving the cost of appraising all the potential acquisitions.

Then Lew Crutcher, Chief of Planning and Design, would carefully estimate the kinds and costs of development, and a resource analysis would indicate the flora and fauna of the area. Only then would Hornbeck take up the desired options to put together a park.

"The unilateral option process was immensely successful," Hornbeck remarks, "and produced lands negotiated for in a friendly way at values which, although they were fair market values, will never be repeated."

Clearly, if any one concept characterizes the District's operations, it is this kind of planning.

istered. This would require about $70 million, including federal and state grants. The District, it was stressed, had ten years at most to acquire parkland needed for the next half century before urban sprawl encroached.

AB 925: A Legislative Milestone

By a five-to-two vote, the Board approved seeking a ten-cent tax increase from the state legislature, and the campaign was begun under the able leadership of Alameda County Supervisor Joseph Bort as Chairman of the Committee for More Parklands. He devoted his considerable skills toward gathering the support of city councils, civic organizations, and key private business representatives in leadership positions in the East Bay. Without his leadership, the tax increase could not have been achieved. The entire campaign was financed by contributor gifts, including substantial sums from most members of the District's Board of Directors and top staff.

"We spent about a year getting support," recalls Bort. "Nobody likes taxes to be raised, and then some people

Endless summer at Crown Memorial State Beach: Catamaran sails are silhouetted against the water as sailing enthusiasts relax after a long day on San Francisco Bay.

thought that we already had plenty of open space, but it was something that had to be done." Still, it was not an easy process.

Before the key legislator, State Assemblyman John Knox, would agree to carry the measure, dubbed AB 925, he required that the District receive a clean bill of health from A. Alan Post, the California legislature's nationally renowned analyst. A two-month study by Post's office ensued, and the District won Post's nod of approval that an increase was needed for an expansion program.

Legislative concurrence required that all 11 state legislators from the District's area support the measure, and this, too, was achieved, thanks in large part to busloads of citizens who journeyed to Sacramento to lobby for the bill.

Compromises were necessary. Achieving the proper balance of funds between acquisition on the one hand and development and operations on the other required all of the District's delicate negotiating skills, but agreement was finally reached on eight cents for acquisition and two cents for development and operation of the newly acquired parklands. Another compromise provided for a referendum procedure "if voters weren't happy with the way things were done."

AB 925 passed in 1971. It proved to be the only bill for a tax increase signed by Governor Ronald Reagan that year.

AB 925, as it turned out, was a milestone in District administration as well as finances. Assemblyman John Knox was instrumental in striking one of the more important compromises of the measure, mandating that the first five-cent increase would become effective in 1972, with the second increase to come only after a new master plan, anticipated for 1974, had been adopted. At the time of AB 925's passage, Trudeau had already begun the master planning process that would guide the District's future thrust in expansion. The Plan would prove to be as important to the District as the bill's provisions for funding.

The Master Plan: "It Works Beautifully!"

The development of the Plan was a remarkable story of cooperative efforts between the District, local governments, and the public. Long-range planning was not a new concept; as far back as 1940 then-General Manager Elbert Vail had outlined his plans for the future. But never had the District tackled such comprehensive strategy decisions.

Seeking the widest possible input and assistance in formulating the Master Plan, General Manager Trudeau brought together the skills of professional planners and the recommendations and experience of District staff and citizens served by the District. Former Secretary of the Interior Stewart Udall and his firm, Overview, were hired to formulate the Plan. The Park District Board, staff, and employees provided recommendations and necessary data. A third element was the local citizenry, working through two organized committees, who would study the proposals and offer their own recommendations.

The first committee, an 83-member Citizens Task Force chaired by Joseph Bort and composed of a broad spectrum of private citizens, made in-depth studies of potential park sites. Larry Milnes, Fremont's Assistant City Manager, chaired the Public Agency Advisory Committee. Local governmental bodies nominated 60 representatives to this committee, which followed closely the work of the Citizens Task Force and acted as liaison with city and county agencies.

A three-way agreement between Overview, the District, and the Association of Bay Area Governments provided for ABAG to fund 75 percent and the District 25 percent of the Master Plan consultant costs. "It was to be the model for developing regional park master plans for other park agencies in the nine-county area," recalls Assistant General Manager Jerry Kent, who worked out the agreement.

An essential contribution of the Citizens Task Force was its formulation of criteria and methodology for parkland acquisition. Much of this work was done by a series of subcommittees.

The Trails Subcommittee, for example, headed by Dr. Glenn Seaborg, Nobel Prize-winning chemist of the Lawrence Berkeley Laboratory, hammered out principles for the building and maintenance of trails. "We came up with a report that included a map of suggested trails in the parks and connecting trails between the parks," remembers Dr. Seaborg. "Our Task Force took exploratory trips to many places—to the Ohlone Wilderness, to Mission Peak. I remember having a picnic supper at Del Valle as part of a weekend trip."

Other Citizens Task Force members formulated criteria for evaluating possible acquisitions: 1) whether they were irreplaceable or irreversible; 2) whether they were in jeopardy; 3) whether they would be useful; 4) whether they were valuable in their present state or should be developed; and 5) the ease of acquiring them. The consultants used these criteria as a guide for their recommendations. "I think the great contribution of Stewart Udall," Task Force member Kay Kerr observes, "was in establishing the outlines in the

Director Howard Cogswell and Assistant General Manager Jerry Kent inspect the restoration at Crown Beach. Acquisition of bayshore parklands was a major arm of the Master Plan.

MISSION PEAK

In preparation for work on the Master Plan, members of the two citizens advisory groups visited every park in the District and other areas being considered for parks. Larry Milnes, who headed the Public Agency Advisory Committee, recalls one trip:

"We drove our automobile caravan to the foot of Mission Peak. Dr. Glenn Seaborg was in my automobile, along with Dr. Howard Cogswell, Dr. Robert Fisher, a local historian, and Margaret Bowman. When we arrived at the foot of Mission Peak, Dr. Seaborg observed that climbing the peak had been one of his life ambi-

tions, and since he was there, he was going to climb to the top. He invited anyone else who might want to go along with him to also make the climb. There was a special pleasure in being able to hike to Mission Peak with Dr. Seaborg, who was the Chairman of the Trails Committee for the Park District and made major contributions to the trail system.

"The view from Mission Peak was really something to behold. You could look down on Fremont and the total Bay Area and see the expanses of dense urbanization, the suburban sprawl. The view from

Mission Peak also offers the opportunity to look down on eagles soaring by.

"Mission Peak has another rather significant place in history. Pete Starr, author of Starr's *Guide to the John Muir Trail and the High Sierra Region*, spent his holiday time as a youngster at the Mission Peak ranch of his grandfather, A.A. Moore."

Where but in the East Bay Regional Park District can you stand on a historic peak, gazing down at eagles, with a bay at your feet and views of forested hills around you?

Building Rome In a Day. This handsome replica of St. Peter's Basilica in Rome won Best of Show in sand castle division at the 1983 Sand Castle and Sand Sculpture Contest at Crown Beach.

Master Plan for where and what would be acquired. How it would be acquired and developed could come later."

Adds Bort, "Rather than designating any particular properties"—thus avoiding the inevitable price escalation—"we divided up the money into four sections—trails, wilderness, active parks, and shorelines—to provide for balanced spending on parklands. It was a unique plan in that we set out the objectives, and then the District acquired the property at the appropriate time."

In its final form, as prepared by staff and the Board using the recommendations of Overview and the citizens committees, the Master Plan designated existing and potential parklands as regional parks, recreational areas, wildernesses, shoreline parks, trails, preserves, and land bank category. The Plan outlined balanced acquisitions to be distributed geographically throughout the District based on population and assessed valuation.

Following the Master Plan guidelines has resulted in a system of parks today that shows a striking balance of all those types of parks. "Anyone in our two counties," points out Chris Nelson, "can find reasonably close to where they live, one of each of those categories. If they want to be with a lot of people, there is a swimming beach down the road, or if they want to go off in a wilderness and look for mountain lion tracks, there is a wilderness park not too far away."

The Master Plan is not only a good plan, it is a useful and well-used one. "It's a plan of implementation," concludes Hulet Hornbeck, "and it works just beautifully!"

Citizen Impact: The PAC

More than just balanced parklands, however, came out of the Master Plan process. For one thing, the Citizens Task Force and the Public Agency Advisory Committee, which added a new dimension to professional planning, evolved into the permanently constituted Park Advisory Committee (PAC), a broadly based 23-member group later enlarged to 33, composed of people appointed by Directors and public agencies of the two counties.

Continuing the work begun by the Task Force, the PAC makes recommendations on a wide spectrum of issues to the Board of Directors for its consideration and official action.

"As an ongoing committee, it is different from committees of other agencies," explains Director Mary Jefferds. "PAC members, representing the public, provide an important element in the three-way balance between Board, staff, and public." Such input and cooperation goes a long way toward preventing the sort of citizen-government confrontations that have plagued public agencies in recent years.

Another area where citizens make valuable contributions to the Park District is in attending Board meetings. "It is an area of controversy sometimes," reflects former Director Howard Cogswell, "but I find that when the citizens are there and they have their say, it is very effective."

Citizens have not only had a voice in policy decisions, they have often made useful specific suggestions. Larry Milnes recalls that during the master planning process, a group from the Citizens Task Force visited the Alameda Creek Quarries to view them and talk about their acquisition. "One lady," he remembers, "suggested that perhaps a creative acquisition plan might be developed whereby there could be a tax advantage for the quarry operator to donate land, and then perhaps the Park District could buy some adjoining property. There would be civic benefits as well as tax benefits then to the donor."

As it turned out, the Alameda County Flood Control and Water Conservation District was interested in the quarries for its water replenishment program, the Park District was interested from the recreational standpoint, and after portions of the quarry were donated to the two agencies by the quarry operators, the agencies executed a joint ownership

This idyllic scene at Alameda Creek Quarries illustrates the potential for transformation of former industrial sites into parklands.

and management agreement and proceeded to purchase jointly the remaining parcels required to complete the park. Today 90 acres are open, offering visitors fishing, picnicking, model boating, and hiking. An additional 367 acres await development.

Point Pinole

Most acquisitions such as Alameda Creek Quarries followed the guidelines of the Master Plan, but even before the Plan was adopted, an opportunity presented itself at Point Pinole that the District could not afford to postpone.

The story of Point Pinole actually dates back to the early '60s, when it was earmarked for a park during the campaign for the annexation of Contra Costa County. It was a choice piece of shoreline—a promontory jutting out into the Bay with scenic views in all directions—but it was owned by Bethlehem Steel, which had purchased it from Atlas Powder Company in the early 1960s. Bethlehem planned to erect an integrated steel mill there. Richmond city officials valued the jobs such a mill would provide more highly than they did a park, and threatened to withdraw their approval of annexation if the District went ahead with proposed plans to acquire the Point. The District—reluctant to endanger the Contra Costa annexation—at the last moment acquiesced.

"I remember we were having a Saturday morning meeting to map campaign strategy for the annexation," recalls Hulet Hornbeck, who, prior to joining staff, was Chairman of the Central Contra Costa Committee. "We had a brochure all ready to be passed out that included Point Pinole as one of the parks the District would develop if Contra Costa County joined. In the middle of the meeting, Dick Trudeau called to say that we could not use the literature, so we quickly had to pull that brochure out of the campaign packets. I remember thinking that we had to always bear in mind the larger goal."

The larger goal was achieved, but only after years of patience and persistence. Trudeau had agreed that the District would not pursue Point Pinole unless Bethlehem Steel first approached the District. Eventually, convinced by the depressed condition of the American steel industry that a steel plant at Point Pinole would be uneconomic, Bethlehem in 1970 made overtures to the District, indicating that they were interested in selling. That same year, the District leased an adjoining 161 acres from the State Lands Commission, which became a mini-park next to Parchester Village.

A view down the rocky beach of Pt. Pinole Regional Shoreline. A park that was long in the making but finally opened in 1973, it includes stunning shoreline areas with meadows, eucalyptus stands, rugged beaches, thriving marshes, spectacular bay views, and a 1,225-foot fishing pier.

85

What followed were months of intense, difficult, and confidential negotiations with Bethlehem, which was reluctant to part with the land for less money than they had paid for it.

At the same time, Trudeau faced the formidable challenge of funding the nearly $6 million the District hoped to pay for the 1,000 acres and 3 1/2 miles of shoreline—the largest dollar amount the District had ever expended for property.

In a masterful piece of coordinating what amounted to a three-ring financial circus, Trudeau succeeded in persuading the state to earmark $1.2 million in Land and Water Conservation funds, negotiating a $3 million loan from the Bank of America at a 3.6 percent rate of interest, and raising over $300,000 in private grants.

The acquisition won the District—and the local citizens' committee, which had provided encouragement and valuable support—top awards from the Bay Area Council in 1973.

POINT PINOLE REGIONAL SHORELINE

"That's the most dramatic land acquisition story I've ever heard," insisted a listener on hearing the story of Point Pinole.

Jutting out into the Bay, with views to north, east, west, and south, with wooded hills and living marshland, Point Pinole was earmarked early on as a desirable Contra Costa County park. But at the time the County annexed to the Park District, Bethlehem Steel Company owned the Point, and county officials wanted the steel plant Bethlehem planned to build there, so plans for a park were withdrawn.

Bethlehem ultimately decided against a plant and approached the District with an offer to sell. Lengthy—and highly confidential—negotiations ensued, which also involved the Urban Land Institute, the State Lands Commission, the city of Richmond, federal Land and Water funds, the State Department of Parks and Recreation, and the Bank of America.

The climax came on the critical day when the Land and Water Conservation Fund grants had to be submitted for approval or they would be lost, and Trudeau needed final word on the sale from Bethlehem.

"Early in the morning," recalls Trudeau, "I was up calling the Bethlehem representative, because we had to have their go-ahead by noon. He said he'd try. I called Hulet Hornbeck and he hurried over to my house. I didn't dare shave with my electric shaver because I didn't want to miss the phone call. We sat there waiting and wondering. At 12:15 p.m. Bethlehem called back and said, 'You've got a deal.'"

With incredible good luck, Trudeau located the necessary people—who were scattered around the Bay Area, Sacramento, and Hawaii—and got them all together on a conference call for the final arrangements.

"It was really a cliffhanger," Trudeau concludes. "If we hadn't gotten the grants, if we hadn't been able to borrow from the bank, if all the circumstances hadn't worked perfectly, we wouldn't have made it. And if we hadn't gotten Point Pinole then, we never would have."

It has become an ideal park, a place of scenic solitude situated in the midst of a densely populated urban area. It was truly a one-of-a-kind acquisition.

It was a major step forward in the new thrust for shoreline acquisition that would characterize the decade.

Miller/Knox Regional Shoreline

But shoreline acquisition posed particularly challenging problems. As in the case of Point Pinole, much of the bayshore was already developed and had been held for many years by commercial and railroad interests. Shoreline land thus bore a higher price per acre than hillside areas.

The Miller/Knox Regional Shoreline, for example, was marshy land along the railroad track that was not only high in price but uninspiring as a potential park. There was, in fact, considerable doubt about whether the District should acquire it at all. (When Assemblyman John Knox threw his support to the project, it was labeled by some Directors as Knox's Folly.) Yet it presented not only scenic views but recreation possibilities greatly needed for the densely urbanized Richmond area.

Local citizens campaigned vigorously for the acquisition. Recalls State Senator John Nejedly, "It was a great community effort. I worked hard on it, and a lot of people in the community did, especially the 'shoreline park ladies.' They wrote a cookbook, and they took public officials and park officials on picnics out there."

When it was finally put together, after years of concerted effort on the part of the community, the state legislature, and the District, it was named for the late Senator George Miller Jr. and Assemblyman John Knox, two of the District's best friends.

Bayshore breezes make kite flying a favorite activity at Miller/Knox Regional Shoreline.

A varied coastline and superb birdwatching are only two of the attractions at San Leandro Bay Regional Shoreline. Visitors may also enjoy the boardwalk into Arrowhead Marsh, a two-lane boat launching ramp, fishing, trails, picnicking, exercise course, and nature study.

San Leandro Bay Regional Shoreline

San Leandro Bay Regional Shoreline was another particularly difficult acquisition, but as it turned out, a spectacularly successful one. Negotiations were complicated because lands had to be leased from Pacific Gas and Electric Company, the Port of Oakland, EBMUD, the city of Oakland, the State Lands Commission, and the Alameda County Flood Control and Water Conservation District. Discussions with the Port of Oakland dragged on for two years, and EBMUD hesitated to give up the shoreline area it owned where the District wanted to put a trail.

The park was opened to the public in 1979, but San Leandro Bay Regional Shoreline is still in the making; it will eventually tie into Crown Memorial State Beach, which was restored after years of studying its eroding beach, and the two together will be one of the most beautiful urban shoreline park areas anywhere in the world.

"I think it will go down in history as comparable to Golden Gate Park or New York's Central Park," believes Director John Leavitt. Located in a densely populated urban area, the beach and trail system offers panoramic views of the Bay, and the variety of recreational activities—from fishing to bird watching—appeals to a broad spectrum of people. "It's a bay within a bay," concludes Leavitt, "and it's truly unique."

Expansion in New Directions

Meanwhile, other shoreline parks were being added to the District's map, including Brooks Island, which had been purchased earlier but held in reserve, and Point Isabel, which was leased from the U.S. Postal Service.

Several new shoreline areas also served to satisfy the District's goal of providing more parks for southern Alameda County and Contra Costa County. Martinez and Antioch Shorelines soon opened along Contra Costa's north shore, while Hayward Shoreline and Oyster Bay offered access to southern Alameda County's western shoreline.

New inland parks also now dotted the map: Mission Peak Regional Preserve, Alameda Creek Quarries Regional Recreation Area, and Tassajara Creek Regional Park in southern Alameda County, and Black Diamond Mines Regional Preserve, Diablo Foothills Regional Park, and Morgan Territory Regional Preserve in Contra Costa County.

Hayward Regional Shoreline in the Making: In 1980 an outer dyke was breached and Bay waters flowed into a 200-acre area bringing renewed life and habitat for aquatic based creatures. Trails and boardwalks allow visitors to explore the rich shoreline environment, which is intended to remain natural.

THE DEL VALLE CAT

Del Valle Regional Park has its own version of the Loch Ness monster, except that once having sunk into the murky depths, the Del Valle creature has never resurfaced.

It happened when the Park District was building a road in the park, using an old Caterpillar tractor. The timeworn machine had a history of locking in neutral and free tracking, and that's exactly what it did when a newly hired operator got onto it.

A short time later, the service yard received a frantic phone call that the Cat was in the water. The operator had managed to jump off and was rescued from the lake by a county sheriff who was fishing nearby on his day off. Mechanic Ron Holden grabbed his diving gear and a fellow worker and hurried out to the reservoir. "The tracks went right down to the edge of the water," he reports, "and you could see them in the hardpan for about five feet out."

Scuba divers searched unsuccessfully, and even an expert bell diver failed to locate the Cat. But when a spot of oil appeared on the other side of the lake, the construction crew rented a magnet and attached a buoy so the divers could try again. Over the weekend, the magnet and buoy were stolen, and the search was called off.

The last heard from this Cat-turned-lake-monster was when another oil slick appeared on the surface several years later, but that remains the only clue to its demise. It's still there under 300 feet of water, unseen, like its counterpart in Loch Ness.

Additional Funding Available

With the rapid growth of the District, General Manager Trudeau sought additional means to make funding available. Working with Sy Greben of the Los Angeles County Park Department, Trudeau rallied citizen support for a bill to provide park and recreation funds to highly populated urban areas throughout the state. The legislation, the Roberti-Z'berg Urban Open-Space and Recreation Program, passed in 1976, was another milestone in the District's ongoing efforts to make its parks more available to lower income urban residents. The District's share of the funds was used primarily for development in such parks as San Leandro Bay and Miller/Knox.

The Trail System: Another First

Both the Master Plan and citizen input had focused the District's attention on another sort of development: a comprehensive trail system. The District had already begun to develop plans for a unique system that would not only crisscross the parks themselves but would also move alongside private properties to connect the string of ridge parks. The District now tackled the challenge in earnest.

Hulet Hornbeck, who as Chief of Land Acquisition would mastermind the project, began by conferring with George Cardinet, a longtime District supporter who had worked for the Contra Costa County annexation. As Legislative Chairman of the State Horsemen's Association, Cardinet was particularly interested in shepherding trail legislation through the state legislature. The two men established the East Bay Area Trails Council to unite all the trail users—horsemen, hikers, and joggers—for strategic planning.

With the Council's help, the District mapped out a system of connecting trails, making it possible to go from park to park and to other public lands without ever leaving Dis-

When the Easy Bay Skyline Trail opened in 1970, it was the first nonfederal United States National Recreation Trail, winding through Chabot and Redwood. It has since been extended and now connects six regional parks, beginning at Wildcat Canyon and progressing through Tilden, Sibley Volcanic, Huckleberry Botanic, Redwood, and Chabot.

HUCKLEBERRY TARTS

A fragile ecosystem, with rare plants like leatherwood and delicious berries that grow along a trail, is still part of the East Bay scene, thanks to Huckleberry Regional Botanic Preserve.

The Huckleberry area has been known since at least 1913. As early as the 1950s, the Park District had been negotiating to acquire it. The price seemed too high, but the talks continued sporadically, while interested citizens wrote letters and the Regional Parks Association published articles.

By the 1970s the District was ready to acquire the trail, but they had in mind only a small area of woods to protect it.

The pressure increased for preservation of the whole ecosystem surrounding the trail. When a would-be developer bulldozed two swaths out of the chaparral, the jig was up.

Aroused citizens organized the Citizens for Urban Wilderness Areas, which brought together over 30 environmental groups, and marched to a Board meeting with Dr. Glenn Seaborg of the University of California Lawrence Berkeley Laboratory at their head. An internationally famous chemist, Dr. Seaborg is also an enthusiastic hiker, and he knew

Huckleberry Trail. His eloquent appeal at the Board meeting spelled out the necessity for a Botanic Preserve.

The clincher came when the formal proceedings ended. Lucretia Edwards, a strong supporter of environmental preservation, presented each member of the Board with a little basket containing a tasty homemade huckleberry tart— made from berries picked along the trail.

In attempting to be all things to all people—long-range planners, as well as present-day caretakers of the District—Board members also are responsive to the citizens, and this time their decision resulted in the delightful Huckleberry Regional Botanic Preserve that surrounds and protects the Huckleberry Trail.

"It's a fantastic place to visit," observes Joyce Burr, one of the most active citizens in support of urban wilderness areas. "You can find something of interest anytime from January to January. There are wonderful places where little mosses grow, and there are the mammoth trees, and there's lovely dirca in the spring with the long yellow blossoms that look like earrings. It's a truly charming place."

trict property. The first step was funding, and for this state legislators like Senator John A. Nejedly provided invaluable support. Federal legislation and the National Symposium on Trails also served to highlight the burgeoning public interest in trails and facilitated the task of raising funds.

Just acquiring the trail rights posed an additional challenge. Proposed routes skirted the backyards of private property owners, navigated city streets and county open spaces, and sometimes crossed over—or went under—interstate highways and public transit ways. That meant negotiating with innumerable property owners—buying nodes and nodules, acquisition chief Hornbeck called it—holding public hearings and appearing before city councils and county supervisors.

In some cases, public utilities controlled prime trail property—power line easements and abandoned railroad tracks formed good corridors—so water districts, utility districts, and flood control districts entered into the negotiations.

The interconnecting trail system linking many of the Regional Parks is shown on the map below.

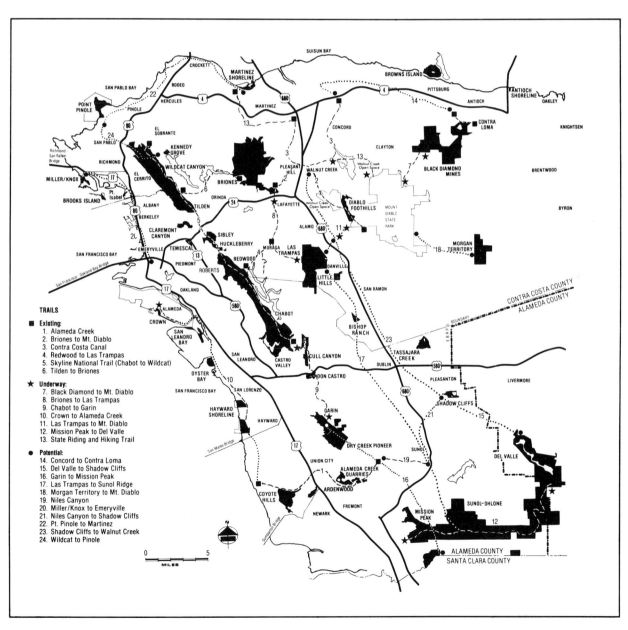

Threading a way through this maze required patience and persistence, but efforts were successful beyond expectations. Almost 100 miles of trails now connect parks with urban areas and transport terminals. "The trails are heavily used," reports Hornbeck, "and the Lafayette/Moraga Trail is the most intensively used of all our parklands in the District."

Interpretive Parks

Meanwhile, developments of a totally different sort were taking place in parks with unusual historic or geographic features that offered opportunities for education and interpretation. These parks with a strong interpretive focus now include Coyote Hills Regional Park, with its 2,300-year-old Indian shell mounds presenting background for studying prehistoric California Indians, and Garin and Dry Creek Pioneer Regional Parks, which offer demonstrations of old-fashioned blacksmithing and other early ranching activities.

One of the most significant interpretive park acquisitions was Black Diamond Mines Regional Preserve, partially purchased in 1975 from the Bureau of Land Management for $2.50 an acre—only after fending off rival claims from a grizzled silica sand miner. Here the public can explore an abandoned silica sand mine and the vestiges of three former coal-mining areas: Somersville, Nortonville, and Stewartville. This was once the largest coal-producing field in California. At Somersville, University of California, Berkeley, archaeologists are conducting one of the most important archaeological digs currently under way in California.

Tilden Merry-Go-Round

In an acquisition of a different sort, the District in 1976 averted a potential crisis at Tilden Park when Harry Perry and his partners announced their intention to sell the merry-go-round. A citizens group, the Save The Merry-Go-Round Committee, immediately petitioned the District to buy the popular attraction.

Since the price proved to be a sticking point, after extensive but unfruitful negotiations the Board approved "friendly" condemnation proceedings, the Contra Costa County Superior Court set a fair price, and the District bought the musical menagerie, with some help from the Committee. The concession is still operated by Harry Perry.

In 1976—merry-go-rounds had captured the public imagination in the 1970s—it was listed in the National Reg-

Learning the survival skills needed by early California Indians is one of the activities fostered by the Parks and Interpretation Department. This tule boat, dubbed Kon Tule I, was built in 1979 at Coyote Hills and paddled across San Francisco Bay. Shown here are District naturalist Jan Southworth, Larry Vojkuska of the San Francisco Bay National Wildlife Refuge, and District naturalist Len Page.

RE-ENACTING HISTORY

At Garin and Dry Creek Pioneer parks, the early days of ranching have been brought to life again. The District's interpretive specialists offer blacksmithing and square dancing activities, as well as exhibits of early farm equipment around the old barn and in other areas of the park.

The first parcels of these historic parks were acquired in the mid-'60s, but one of the crucial areas was the Dry Creek Pioneer ranch owned by three sisters, Mildred, Jeanette, and Dr. Edith Meyers. Then-General Manager William Penn Mott began negotiations with them, taking along as a conversation piece some of his homemade jelly concocted from edible berries of a wild plant. The three sisters had already drafted wills deeding much of their acreage to the Park District, and when the land was threatened with the intrusion of a state highway through the middle of it, the District backed up the sisters in their successful fight against it.

Talks continued sporadically throughout the '60s and '70s until General Manager Richard Trudeau, convinced of the value to the public of the ranchland, made a determined effort and successfully negotiated an agreement with A. Hubbard Moffitt, Jr., attorney for the Meyers sisters. The sisters deeded 1,200 acres to the District for immediate possession, retaining title to their rustic 79-year-old cottage and surrounding acreage, and the District made the most of the area's human and natural history with trails, nature study, and interpretive programs.

"One thing leads to another," muses Dick Trudeau thoughtfully on the many years needed to acquire these parks, "and you build gradually." The result of such patient efforts was a park that re-creates a nearly forgotten way of life.

ister of Historic Places, and with the help of an enthusiastic citizens' campaign and grant money, was restored to its original beauty.

The Art of Acquisition: Cooperation

The rapid escalation of acquisitions meant that Hulet Hornbeck, Chief of Land Acquisition, soon developed to a fine art the increasingly complicated process of putting together parks. Methods included purchases, leases, gifts, bequests, occasional condemnation, and various combinations of these. Usually lengthy and sometimes delicate negotiations were required with a wide variety of public agencies, private developers, individual owners, and entrenched commercial interests.

BLACK DIAMOND MINES REGIONAL PRESERVE

Coal mining in Contra Costa County? Hardly a likely sounding prospect, but a century ago it was a thriving industry, and the East Bay Regional Park District is preserving its remains at one of its most unusual facilities: Black Diamond Mines Regional Preserve, on the flanks of Mt. Diablo.

The Black Diamond story is not only a fascinating glimpse into local history but also an example of the District's persistence and success in overcoming seemingly endless obstacles to park development.

Coal mining began in 1855 on the site of what is now the Preserve, and it soon became California's largest coal-mining operation. Six towns sprang up in the area, of which Somersville and Nortonville were the largest, each with a peak population of about 1000—mostly Welsh and Irish miners.

More than a dozen underground mines flourished, producing a low-grade coal that was used for fuel in homes, mills, and steamboats as far away as Sacramento and Stockton.

Mining activity peaked in the 1870s, but higher quality coal from other areas, plus rising mining costs, eventually drove the mines out of business. By the time the last mine closed in 1902, 4 million tons of coal, valued at $20 million, had been taken out of the ground.

In 1922 underground mining began again near the long-abandoned Somersville and Nortonville townsites. This time the product was high-quality silica sand, which was used nearby for glassmaking and for foundry casting. Visitors can still see the even rows of rooms from which the sandstone was removed, alternating with rows of rock pillars left to support the mine roof.

Competition from other sources and the closing of the foundry forced the closing of the sand mines by 1949, by which time more than one million tons of sand had been removed. The area then reverted to grazing.

In 1975 the District—after successfully overcoming competing claims for the mineral rights from a modern-day would-be silica sand miner—acquired 360 acres from the Bureau of Land Management. Additional parcels were purchased during the 1970s and 1980s to form the 3,809-acre Preserve of today.

Preparations for public access began immediately, but as is sometimes the case with its acquisitions, the District first had to overcome troubles that came with the territory. In this instance, it was abandoned mine shafts, which posed severe hazards and had already claimed a number of lives.

Locating the openings was a prodigious task in itself—records had long since been destroyed—and required a ground search by teams of men (and a specially trained dog) who sometimes had to drag themselves on their stomachs through dense underbrush to find the telltale ventilator shafts.

The openings then had to be sealed with special closures that would minimize disturbance to the local wildlife and would also discourage vandalism by area youngsters who had torn down earlier closures.

Plans were then implemented for guided public tours through one of the silica sand mine shafts and for historical resurrection of the activities of the area, possibly making one of the nearby towns into a living history museum. With this in mind, the Park District agreed to allow Archaeology Professor James Deetz of the University of California, Berkeley, to engage his students in an historical dig at the site of Somersville.

At the same time, an annual celebration of the area's history was also launched. Dubbed Black Diamond Days, it offers a living history program recreating local town life in the coal mining heyday, with Welsh dancers, old-timers' reminiscences, and exhibits of long-forgotten mining techniques.

But no sooner had these programs of tours, digs, and celebrations become established than Mother Nature threw the park a curve ball. The severe rains of the winter of 1983 set off unprecedented landslides at Black Diamond

At Black Diamond Mines a silica sand mine is open for public tours. Here naturalist Joanne Dean and General Manager Richard Trudeau are checking the mine walls with flashlights.

which caused extensive damage to the park's only access road and to the mines, and exposed a Southern Pacific Pipe Line Company fuel pipeline, which cracked and spilled a small amount of high test fuel. As a result, the park was temporarily closed to visitors. Lengthy and difficult negotiations between SPPL and the District ensued, with former state legislators John Knox and John Nejedly assisting the District.

At a dramatic meeting of the Board of Directors held July 19, 1983, attended by over 100 citizens expressing concern about damage to the park, SPPL announced it would relocate the pipeline entirely out of the park and would also regrade roads, remove or bury pipeline segments, and re-seed disturbed ground.

With these assurances, the District was able to reopen the park in July 1983. Tours of the silica sand mine resumed in August, and the District could once again proceed with its plan to develop more elaborate mine tours for the future.

Thanks to strong cooperation among government agencies, private citizens, industry, and the District, Black Diamond now boasts one of the most unusual facilities and interpretive programs in the area, and when the park is completed, it will be a full reflection of both the vision and persistence that have characterized District acquisitions from the very beginning.

Cotton candy and a sandy beach are big attractions at Shadow Cliffs, a former quarry donated to the Park District by Kaiser Industries.

Take Shadow Cliffs, for example, which involved the complex issue of gifts. When Kaiser Sand and Gravel Division of Kaiser Industries donated the land at what became Shadow Cliffs Regional Recreation Area in 1969, the Park District formed the Inter-County Parks Foundation as a tax-exempt, nonprofit foundation to facilitate such gifts of money and land. Then, in a unique procedure, the value of the land at Shadow Cliffs was matched by a federal Land and Water Conservation Fund grant for development. With it, the District turned a stark, depleted quarry into a state design award-winning swimming area with a beach, year-round fishing, picnicking, and ultimately a giant waterslide.

That kind of joint agreement between private citizens, industry, the District, and governmental agencies, which serves the best interests of the public at the same time as it reflects the goals of all concerned, became increasingly common as the land acquisition program grew more complex.

In a formidable example of such cooperative efforts, the District chiseled out the Briones to Mt. Diablo Trail as a joint project with three cities and funded it with local, state, and federal monies. Other inter-agency arrangements have been made with the California Conservation Corps and CETA (Comprehensive Employment and Training Act) for maintenance workers.

Cooperation, of course, requires compromise, and the District was adept at working out such agreements, successfully negotiating the move of visible high-voltage power lines in Briones Regional Park, the removal of county roads that bisected parks, and the protection from housing developers of recreation area land leased from the Flood Control District. In order to strengthen its authority in situations such as these, the District successfully sponsored state legislation establishing "rebuttable presumption." This doctrine required that any intrusion on owned or leased regional park property, such as roads, would have to be proven to be of equal or higher use than parklands before it could be approved.

Innovations to Meet New Challenges

The demands of the rapid expansion of the 1970s also required a more systematic management structure, which Trudeau had anticipated at the time the Master Plan was adopted. In 1974, the Board commissioned Arthur Young and Company to undertake a management study, and the District, as a result, began setting up its organizational development and training program.

This eucalyptus grove provides a quiet counterpoint to the fast-paced urban life nearby.

The same year the District became involved in what would become a major issue of the 1970s and 1980s—equal employment opportunity—when it adopted an Affirmative Action Program with a manual of procedures developed by employees, union representatives, and local citizens representing labor, minority groups, women's groups, and business interests.

By 1983, the goals of population parity—the proper percentage of each ethnic group and of women according to the Alameda and Contra Costa counties work forces—had been reached. An example of the innovative programs necessary to accomplish the goal is the craft apprenticeship training, which results in state-sanctioned diplomas for carpenters, mechanics, painters, and heavy equipment operators. The first three journeypersons graduated in 1983.

Not all developments, however, were as smooth, and the tumultuous growth of the early 1970s brought its share of growing pains. One of the more wrenching was a two-month employee strike from April to June of 1975—the only one ever in District history. At issue was who would stay in the union's bargaining unit and who would become part of the management team to guide the District in the 1970s and 1980s. During the strike, the parks were kept open by 18 management employees.

Throughout this period of management growth, labor unrest, and change in District work force, the District worked to develop an organizational style that would satisfy employees' desire to be involved in project-oriented field work, yet insure that all the specialized aspects of administration were accomplished. The result was a unique management cycle system including formal, detailed job descriptions, goal-setting, modified zero-base budgeting, professional construction management, and greater citizen and employee participation in decisions.

As these management changes were being implemented, General Manager Trudeau moved to apply equally sophisti-

Participants in Hike-A-Nation here enjoy the Regional Parks as they hike through on their way from the West Coast to Washington, D.C. The group of hikers from throughout the U.S. made the cross-country trek in the summer of 1980 to demonstrate the need for a national east-west trail system.

cated principles to assessing the District's overall performance. A longtime advocate of professionally conducted studies, he recommended that the Board hire the Tyler Research Corporation in 1976 to survey District residents to determine their level of satisfaction with District programs and their suggestions for change. The study, which included a broad sample of resident contacts, reported an overwhelming 94 percent user satisfaction and estimated the number of visitors at over 10 million. The most frequent suggestion for change: more recreational facilities.

Two years later, seeking to quantify the District's contribution to the East Bay, Trudeau commissioned a graduate student in economics at the University of California, Berkeley, to conduct an economic study. "Parks provide opportunities for recreation, relaxation, and preservation of the environment," he explains, "but we felt that they were justifiable economically also."

This proved to be the case. The study showed that for almost every dollar received in taxes or grants, the District returned three to the community in primary or secondary benefits, in addition to the social benefits and the contribution made to a better quality of life for area residents.

Public Safety: A Prime Concern

High satisfaction and economic benefits were one side of the coin of greatly increased park usage; the other was the problems inherent in handling the millions of visitors now flocking to the facilities in a decade when vandalism, alcohol, and drugs were more and more commonplace. Public safety—always a prime concern—required more careful and specialized attention.

In the early days, park workers doubled as rangers, carrying badges in their pockets which they donned to stop speeding cars. By the 1970s, the Public Safety Officers, as they were called, had become a trained, professional group who had a tough job to do and did it well. The arrival of the District's own helicopter in August 1973 meant that increased surveillance and rescue work was possible over parklands that were scattered throughout the 1,289 square miles of the District's jurisdiction.

"We have established an enviable record in providing public safety," observes Director Harlan Kessel. "It is a notable achievement that no area of the park system has ever been allowed to become a hangout and staging area for crime, drugs, and violence. But we must continue to be aware that there is nothing worse for parks and the open space movement than to lack public protection."

Eagle II, the District's Hughes 500C helicopter, patrols daily, providing police, fire, and rescue services for the parks and neighboring communities.

The Eucalyptus Freeze

Mother Nature, however, was not making the job of protecting the public any easier. The particularly severe winter of 1972, which brought snow and freezing temperatures to the usually temperate Bay Area, wreaked havoc on the eucalyptus trees, which had been growing profusely since the 1920s when seedlings from Australia were planted. Vast acres of the stately trees died, creating a fire hazard of monumental proportions along the East Bay ridgeline. The District desperately appealed to the federal government for funding for a systematic fire prevention program, but the resulting bill, carried by Senator Alan Cranston, failed by only 34 votes. Some financial aid became available when California declared a state of emergency in the areas affected by the freeze, and Washington eventually provided a $2 million allocation for removing dead trees and constructing fuel breaks.

Firefighters at work: In a 1983 experimental program designed to reduce fire hazards in the parks, a herd of over 250 goats was put to work browsing along fuel breaks in the parks.

102

Under the Adopt-A-Park plan, industry lends a helping hand to the residents of the Easy Bay. Here executives and employees of Kaiser Aluminum & Chemical Corporation help put together a playground for Roberts Recreation Area.

Proposition 13

Despite the problems posed by freezes, vandalism, and other disasters, by 1978 the District was well on the way to fulfilling the charges of the Master Plan and restructuring its operations to cope with the ongoing expansion.

But in 1978 that growth was brought to a sudden standstill with the passage of Proposition 13, the first salvo in a rising California taxpayers' revolt against high property taxes. The measure, which dramatically reduced property taxes, undermined the District's secure financial foundation.

The crisis called on all of Trudeau's innovative problem-solving skills. Although some money still came from the state, the District would have to reorder its funding totally.

The District began a search for innovative ideas and new sources of funds, while a rigorous regimen of belt-tightening was instituted which in 1979 alone cut $1 million in operating expenses. Within the next two years, Trudeau initiated the Adopt-A-Park program, whereby private industry agreed to assist a designated park with funds and labor.

Another hopeful source was grant money, which would enable the District to maintain its facilities and build new ones. At Tilden's Environmental Education Center, for example, a donation of $10,000 from the Oakland Lions Club was matched by $10,500 from Mervyn's Department Stores for initial design of the Nocturnal Animal Hall, and $8,280 for laboratory-classroom construction was funded by Chevron U.S.A.

103

The Environmental Education Center, first of the District's interpretive centers, offers such diverse activities as puppet shows, Japanese paper folding, slide shows, story telling, exhibits, and naturalist-led nature walks.

As a stopgap measure to keep projects in process alive, Trudeau succeeded in adding major funding for the District to an Assembly financial package bill. The bill proposed using California offshore oil money from the Energy and Resources Fund—money which had traditionally gone to the schools—for park projects. In a last-minute compromise, Trudeau persuaded the University of California to remain neutral, and the bill passed. "We got money for a lot of projects in that bill," reports Trudeau. "I think we got more out of it than any other agency except for the state."

Trudeau and staff found other new ways of accomplishing the impossible. "You need to work with property developers," Trudeau emphasizes, "to achieve open space and find ways that will benefit them." At Coyote Hills Regional Park, for example, a quarry operator donated land and developed it to the District's specifications in return for support for his project. Developers of new homes at Ridgemont, high in the Oakland hills, have added a park-like setting to their homesites by donating the open space land to the Park District. And when a new proposal to quarry Apperson Ridge came from Ed De Silva, along with plans for mitigation, the District was able to work out a satisfactory agreement.

By developing these new resources, the District could continue its land acquisition program, adding to existing trails and parks such as Claremont Canyon Regional Preserve and acquiring new ones such as Ardenwood Regional Preserve. "We've been remarkably successful, with proper

The Patterson Mansion is a unique feature of Ardenwood Regional Preserve. When fully developed, Ardenwood will preserve and demonstrate historical and current farming techniques.

management, in weathering Proposition 13," comments Director Walter Costa.

As further indication that Proposition 13 had not permanently cramped the District's style, the U.S. Department of the Interior bestowed its coveted Outdoor Recreation Achievement Award on the District in 1979.

Master Plan, 1980

Nevertheless, the drastic changes in funding sources occasioned by Proposition 13, and the new perspectives of the 1970s that brought increased awareness of the values of parklands, trails, and open space, necessitated updating the 1973 Master Plan. The Park Advisory Committee, District staff, the Board, and the public, after extensively reviewing the original Plan, formulated a revised Plan that was approved by the Board in 1980.

As President of the Board at that time, Mary Lee Jefferds wrote: "Master Plan 1980 identifies goals, defines procedures, and provides comprehensive guidelines for implementation. This document serves as a blueprint guiding our practical decisions in prudent financing, acquisitions, capital development, and land use planning."

The Plan assures protection of the East Bay's natural resources; less than 10 percent of the total inventory of the District's parklands will be developed, and the other 90 percent will be left in a natural condition. Each parkland has its own balance, and the overall areas provide both a geographical balance and a selection of each of the primary categories: recreational areas, parks, wilderness, shorelines, preserves, trails, and land bank. In addition, the Plan provides for continual review by the Park Advisory Committee, the Board of Directors, and the public.

Accommodation and Compromise

The District continues to remain responsive to community concerns. Toward the end of the 1970s, with growing public awareness of the need to conserve energy, the District developed an energy conservation manual and installed a solar energy system, donated by Pacific Gas and Electric Company, for the bathhouse at the Contra Loma Regional Park's beach.

Shortly thereafter, at Briones, the largest of the regional parks, the District successfully concluded a troublesome 12-year feud over planned recreational use of the northern end of the park. Reacting to the community's need for recreational facilities, the District had originally proposed a major development plan for that area, but the proposal had aroused

the ire of local homeowners, who feared increased traffic, noise, and intrusion on their quiet neighborhood.

With the assistance of an environmental mediator from the University of Washington called in by the District, a compromise was ultimately reached. The protesters agreed to an access road plus low-key, limited recreational use—hiking, picnicking, and nature study—in the north end of the park, with the major recreational development focused in the southern part of the park.

In another milestone of compromise and negotiation, the District in 1982 signed a precedent-setting, 10-year lease agreement with the San Francisco Water Department enabling the District to open a 21-mile trail traversing Water Department land in southern Alameda County. The hiking and equestrian trail, which will wind over high, undulating land, interspersed with ponds and forests, will link Mission Peak Regional Preserve with Del Valle Regional Park.

A major problem in the negotiations—compatibility of recreational and water conservation uses—was solved by making the parcels of property wide enough to provide "insulation" and lessen chances of trespassing onto Water Department lands.

Sailboats at Del Valle Regional Park (opposite page) and the barn at the Little Farm in Tilden Park show the variety of activities visitors can find in the Regional Parks.

At Black Diamond Mines Regional Preserve, winter storms of 1983 washed out the access road and severely damaged a Southern Pacific Pipe Line Company fuel pipeline within the park.

Mother Nature Strikes Again

But one force with which there was no compromise was Mother Nature, who dealt the area—and the entire country—two winters in a row of devasting storms and floods in 1982 and 1983. This came only four years after two years of severe drought in 1977 and 1978.

Unusually heavy rains in the winter of 1982, and the ensuing floods and landslides, caused $1.3 million worth of damage to the District's parks. Landslides in Tilden Park, for example, closed Cañon Drive, which provides access to Berkeley, and debris was deposited in Lake Temescal, undoing much of the dredging work accomplished in 1978 and 1979. At the same time, Del Valle reservoir overflowed its banks, spreading debris and washing out campsites and roads.

The storms of 1983 compounded the damage, since the ground was already saturated. This time the losses totaled $1.5 million and forced the temporary closing of Del Valle Regional Park, where electrical service was knocked out; Black Diamond Mines Regional Preserve, where landslides washed out the only access road and severely damaged a high pressure jet fuel pipeline; and various sections of roads and trails in Tilden, Wildcat Canyon, and Briones Regional Parks and the Lafayette/Moraga Trail.

Repairing the damages, while at the same time moving forcefully to implement its expansion plans, calls on all the resourcefulness the District can muster and proves the agency's strength developed over the last five decades.

The Board of Directors

An important element in the District's strength and adaptability has been—and continues to be—its Board of Directors, which has kept pace with changing times and challenges. Since 1964 Directors have been elected from wards instead of at large, and they have brought to the District not only area-wide representation but also a variety of skills and interests to match the District's wide variety of needs. One director followed the financial situation with meticulous care, while another dealt capably with government officials. They listened and weighed the opinions of all those who were concerned: citizens, staff, employees, legislators, and local public officials. When one director opened office hours on Friday afternoons and nobody came to him, he gathered up his dog-and-pony show and took the parks to the public, speaking at luncheons, schools, and club meetings. It was typical of the dedication of Board members.

Dedication is, in fact, a hallmark of the District's entire operation, from Board to management to staff and employees. "I am greatly impressed by the incredible array of talent and skills that comes to us in support of our activities," comments Director Ted Radke. His observation is seconded by fellow Director Harlan Kessel. "Compared to other systems," Kessel remarks, "the quality of professional achievement of District staff is truly notably superior." Recognition for the District's performance comes from all over the country as well, and the walls at the District's Oakland headquarters are dotted with awards and plaques from federal, state, and local governments and organizations.

Fifty Years of Growth

By the beginning of 1984, the District included 41 parks totaling 57,000 acres, serving more than 15 million visitors. "It is quite significant," Director Walter Costa points out, "that in just a six-year period of time the District has increased by 20,000 acres—a 33 percent jump."

The last two decades of growth, which occurred at a time when land acquisition had to happen then or not at all, can be ascribed to outstanding efforts on the part of the general managers and staff, a Board that was not only sympathetic to land acquisition but pushing for it, and an active and concerned citizenry who are environmentally aware and dedicated to the protection and development of the District. "The foundation of parks is land," maintains Director Lynn Bowers, sounding the keynote theme for the District's next half century, "and our challenge is to identify the best potential parklands and acquire them as soon as possible." Director John O'Donnell concurs, adding that the District must also concentrate on "building up what we already have."

At the brink of its second half century, the Park District is poised for continued dramatic growth. "The District probably will surpass any urban area in the United States for parkland in the next couple of years," predicts Hulet Hornbeck confidently, "even in the face of more limited resources."

And the District is still, as it always has been, one of a kind in many ways: unique in topography, in connecting hilltops with shorelines by trails, in the leadership roles it has taken in state and federal government relationships and in interaction with the public.

"We like to be in the forefront," insists Richard Trudeau. "We like to be first if we can."

His efforts, and those of the Board, staff, and concerned residents of the District, ensure that they will be.

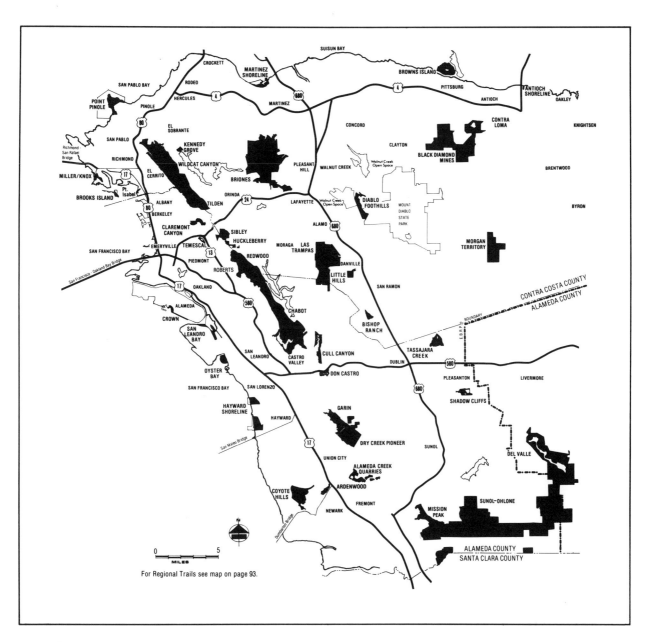

Map shows District in 1984 on its 50th Anniversary.

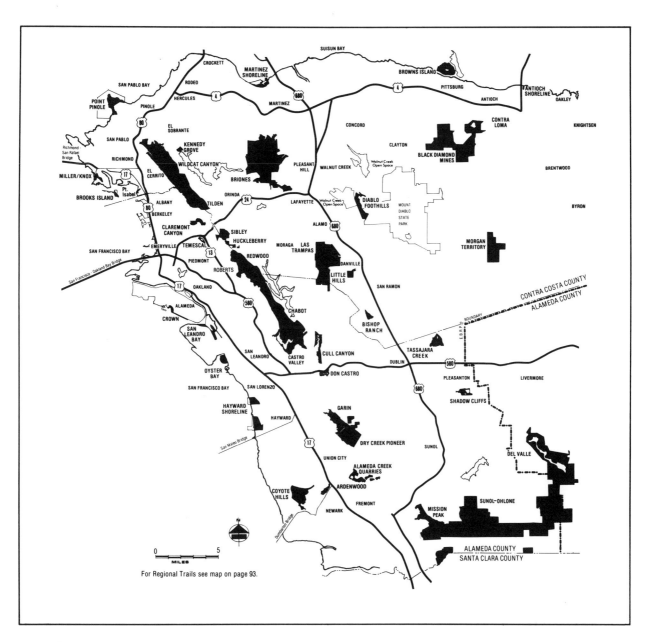

Map shows District in 1984 on its 50th Anniversary.

*I hold that man is
in the right who is most closely
in league with the future.*
—Henrik Ibsen

Epilogue

A View to the Future

It was the year 1934, the heart of the Great Depression. A group of public-spirited "futurists" met, discussed and then created what is now the universally respected and acclaimed East Bay Regional Park District.

Fifty years have passed. Fifty years of social and political turmoil—world war; emergence of new world powers; the civil rights movement; new and changing roles for government. Remarkably, however, the founders' ideas and plans have admirably stood the test of time and truly the charter laid down by them effectively anticipated and carved out a role of consequence for the District. Respect and reverence for the physical environment, paralleled by a determination to interpret this environment in a positive way to an emerging urban population became the lasting goals of the District—and the fact that these parallel needs retain their meaning and vitality today is indicative that the direction taken by District founders was well-chosen and remarkably visionary.

It is now the year 1984 and District leadership—Board and staff—is challenged to maintain the quality of "futurist" decision-making in order to provide the proper parks, recreation and environmental direction for the next 50 years and beyond. The complexity of the task predictably will match at least that which faced the Founders. Part of that complexity assuredly can be identified and responded to. Just as certain, however, is the fact that an imposing array of complex societal issues and problems, presently unknown or unclear, are likely to arise as the District embarks upon the second fifty years of its history.

Preservation of Parks and Open Space Lands

Much of the area now served by the District is urbanized. It is reasonable to assume that further urban impact will continue to occur in the East Bay region. Inevitably this trend will complicate the task of acquiring and properly maintaining those needed open spaces which are a vital ingredient in positive, healthy human life. This is because lands which provide excellent park and open space sites frequently have distinctive potential for residential and other use. Also, profit-making organizations engaged in property acquisition and development will remain a competitive factor in determining how land will be used and what remains available for parks. Further, as urbanization expands and intensifies, those lands already acquired for park and open space purpose inevitably will become targets for non-recreational development.

The District must continue to view acquisition and preservation of parks and open space lands as a matter of primary responsibility. Lands identified and chosen for this use must be judiciously and intelligently selected, in terms of their ecological and human service, as well as significance. The District will continue to use a wide assortment of joint funding strategies in order to reduce the burden of cost to the local property taxpayer. As in the past, new and innovative techniques involving legislation, partnerships, and no fee or low fee acquisition, will be created, always with the view in mind of retaining the integrity of the District's overall goals.

As an adjunct to the effort of preserving land, interpretive programs will be a high priority, partly for their intrinsic value to human beings, but also as a means of encouraging the general public to recognize and respect the values of park and open space.

Service to Urban Populations

With the passage of time the "public" served by the District has experienced a rather remarkable change. Similar to urbanization found in other high-density areas of the United States, the District's "majority" now includes some special populations with particular needs and identification—i.e. older Americans, physically and/or emotionally disabled, ethnic minorities, single parents, latchkey children, and

114

new immigrants. Most demographic experts are convinced that this emergence of special populations will be a factor of major consequence in the foreseeable future. Thus, the District's task includes a profound responsibility to accommodate the needs of these groups, as well as to encourage the kinds of appreciation and understanding which will assist each special population to enjoy and properly use the lands. With this responsibility comes the recognition that for a variety of reasons such as physical disability, financial limits, age, and lack of privately-owned transportation, many urban citizens cannot normally enjoy the benefits of the system. In a spirit of service and egalitarianism the District will accept the extra burden and special challenge to understand these impediments in order to maximize the means by which all citizens can be served.

Leisure Demands

There exists much reliable data about the growing significance of leisure time in the lives of citizens. Certainly the commercial implications of leisure, as an industry, are well-documented, but perhaps more important is the fact that even in periods of economic recession and depression the citizens' interest in leisure activities continues to expand and tends to incorporate new directions.

For East Bay Regional Park District, this emergence of leisure as a major force poses all types of profound challenges. In the years ahead, the District will assume an ever-larger stewardship role in increasing availability of leisure experience and will develop new techniques for informing the public in such a manner as to encourage their participation. At this time, the following considerations are important:

> More urban people will live in multiple dwelling settings. Availability of urban open spaces and parks thus becomes a matter of heightened importance.

> Factors of energy conservation, cost of public transportation, lack of available private transportation, etc., suggest a greater need for parks located in proximity to urban centers.

> More and more of the urban population, particularly adults, have relatively sedentary professional and wage-earning activities. This produces a need for physical exercise. People will seek an attractive outdoor environment for this.

Assuredly in the years ahead, experience will provide further clarification of the District's responsibility for meeting leisure needs.

The Staff

East Bay Regional Park District has been fortunate in its ability to attract and retain a staff of great commitment and vigor, dedicated to a concept of public service. This did not happen by accident; rather it reflects the recognition by Board and management that an effective staff which is properly recognized and rewarded is a major key to achieving overall objectives.

To continue this, it is essential that the District provide general employment conditions conducive to retaining current staff as well as attractive to qualified new employees.

As the next fifty years is addressed in terms of staffing considerations, management will be conscious of the need to selectively avail itself of the values of mechanization and computer technology. Employees will be encouraged and assisted in the effort to broaden their sense of overall responsibility and mission. Recognition of the potential values of entrepreneurial skills allied with park sensitivities will be stressed, and staff development will recognize the importance of understanding urban society and urban populations.

The efforts in achieving an effective affirmative action program will be maintained, using and stressing training as a basis for promotion. New employment concepts must be introduced when appropriate.

Conclusion—And a New Beginning

Each person intimately involved with the affairs of the District is delighted with the sense of public service and accomplishment that has been experienced, and yet at the same time, humbled at the knowledge of what remains to be accomplished. Some of the future tasks and problems are already known. Assuredly, however, much of what will confront the District in the future can only be speculated.

It is certain that the District has a true sense of mission and that the Board and staff will continue to invest all of their collective energy into the task of achieving this mission, with integrity. Further, citizens will continue to be involved—both through formalized as well as informal channels, to assist, counsel and provide direction.

Staff believes this is a proper, reasonable basis for hope and optimism.

Appendix

EAST BAY REGIONAL PARK DISTRICT
Board of Directors

	Term of Office
Charles Lee Tilden	1939–1950
Leroy Goodrich	1939–1963
August Vollmer	1939–1940
Tommy Roberts	1939–1958
Dr. Aurelia Reinhardt	1939–1945
Emery Stone	1940–1948
John A. Macdonald	1945–1972
Robert Sibley	1948–1958
Milton C. Godfrey	1950–1954
John J. Mulvany	1954–1962
Dr. Robert G. Sproul	1958–1967
Clyde R. Woolridge	1958–1976
George C. Roeding, Jr.	1962–1970
Marlin W. Haley	1963–1974
Mary Helen Calfee	1964
John S. Bryant	1964
Paul J. Badger	1965–1978
Fred C. Blumberg	1965–1977
James H. Corley	1967
Paul E. Harberts	1968–1972
Dr. Howard L. Cogswell	1971–1982
Mary Lee Jefferds	1972–Present
John J. Leavitt	1972–Present
William F. Jardin	1974–1982
Harlan Kessel	1976–Present
Walter H. Costa	1977–Present
Ted Radke	1979–Present
Dr. Donald G. Holtgrieve	1982
Lynn Bowers	1983–Present
John O'Donnell	1983–Present

117

EAST BAY REGIONAL PARK DISTRICT
General Managers

Elbert Vail 1934–1942
August Vollmer 1942
Harold L. Curtiss 1942–1945
Charles Lee Tilden 1945
Richard Walpole 1945–1960
Wesley Adams 1960–1962
William Penn Mott, Jr. 1962–1967
Irwin Luckman 1967–1968
Richard C. Trudeau 1969–Present

EAST BAY REGIONAL PARK DISTRICT
Current Top Management

Richard C. Trudeau; General Manager
Jerry D. Kent; Assistant General Manager
Robert N. Owen; Chief, Administration
Hulet C. Hornbeck; Chief, Land Acquisition
Linda L. Chew; Chief, Development & Public Information
Lewis P. Crutcher; Chief, Planning & Design
Edward J. Loss; Controller
O. Christian Nelson; Chief, Parks & Interpretation
Lawrence G. Olson; Chief, Public Safety
Karen Weber; Personnel Manager

Index

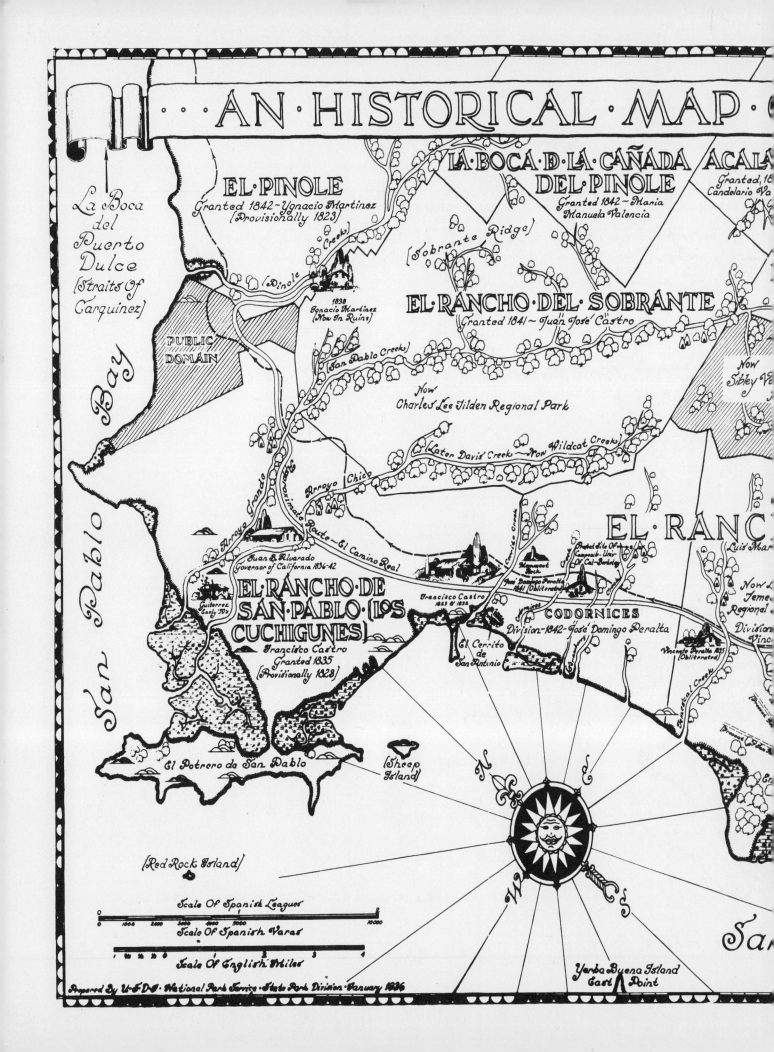

... AN · HISTORICAL · MAP ·

La Boca del Puerto Dulce (Straits Of Carquinez)

EL · PINOLE
Granted 1842 ~ Ygnacio Martinez
(Provisionally 1823)

(Creek)

(Dinole

1838
*Ignacio Martinez
(Now In Ruins)*

PUBLIC DOMAIN

San Pablo Bay

San Pablo Creek)

Arroyo Grande

Approximate Route ~ El Camino Real

Arroyo Chico

*Juan B. Alvarado
Governor of California 1836-42*

*Guiterrez
Early 70's*

EL · RANCHO · DE · SAN · PABLO · [LOS CUCHIGUNES]
*Francisco Castro
Granted 1835
(Provisionally 1828)*

El Potrero de San Pablo

(Sheep Island)

(Red Rock Island)

LA · BOCA · D · LA · CAÑADA **ACALA**
DEL · PINOLE
Granted 1842 ~ Maria
Manuela Valencia

Granted, 1
Candelario Va

(Sobrante Ridge)

EL · RANCHO · DEL · SOBRANTE
Granted 1841 ~ Juan José Castro

Now
Sibley Va

*Now
Charles Lee Tilden Regional Park*

(Later Davis Creek ~ Now Wildcat Creek)

EL · RANC
(Luis Mar

*Probable Site Of
Campanile ~ Univ
Of Cal-Berkeley*

*Monument
Rock*

Now L
Teme
Regional

*José Domingo Peralta
1841 (Obliterated)*

*Francisco Castro
1823 & 1838*

CODORNICES
Division-1842 ~ José Domingo Peralta

*Vincente Peralta 1835
(Obliterated)*

Division
Vinc

*El Cerrito
de San Antonio*

Schnellwal Creek

Scale Of Spanish Leagues

1000 2000 3000 4000 5000   10000

Scale Of Spanish Varas

Scale Of English Miles

Prepared By U·S·D·I · National Park Service · State Park Division · January 1936

*Yerba Buena Island
East Point*

San